Presidential Puzzlers

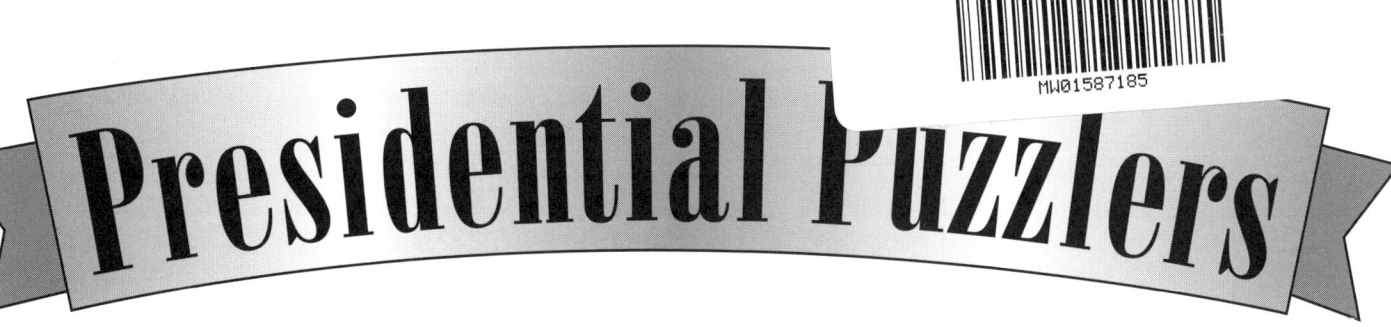

Jeanne Cheyney and Arnold Cheyney

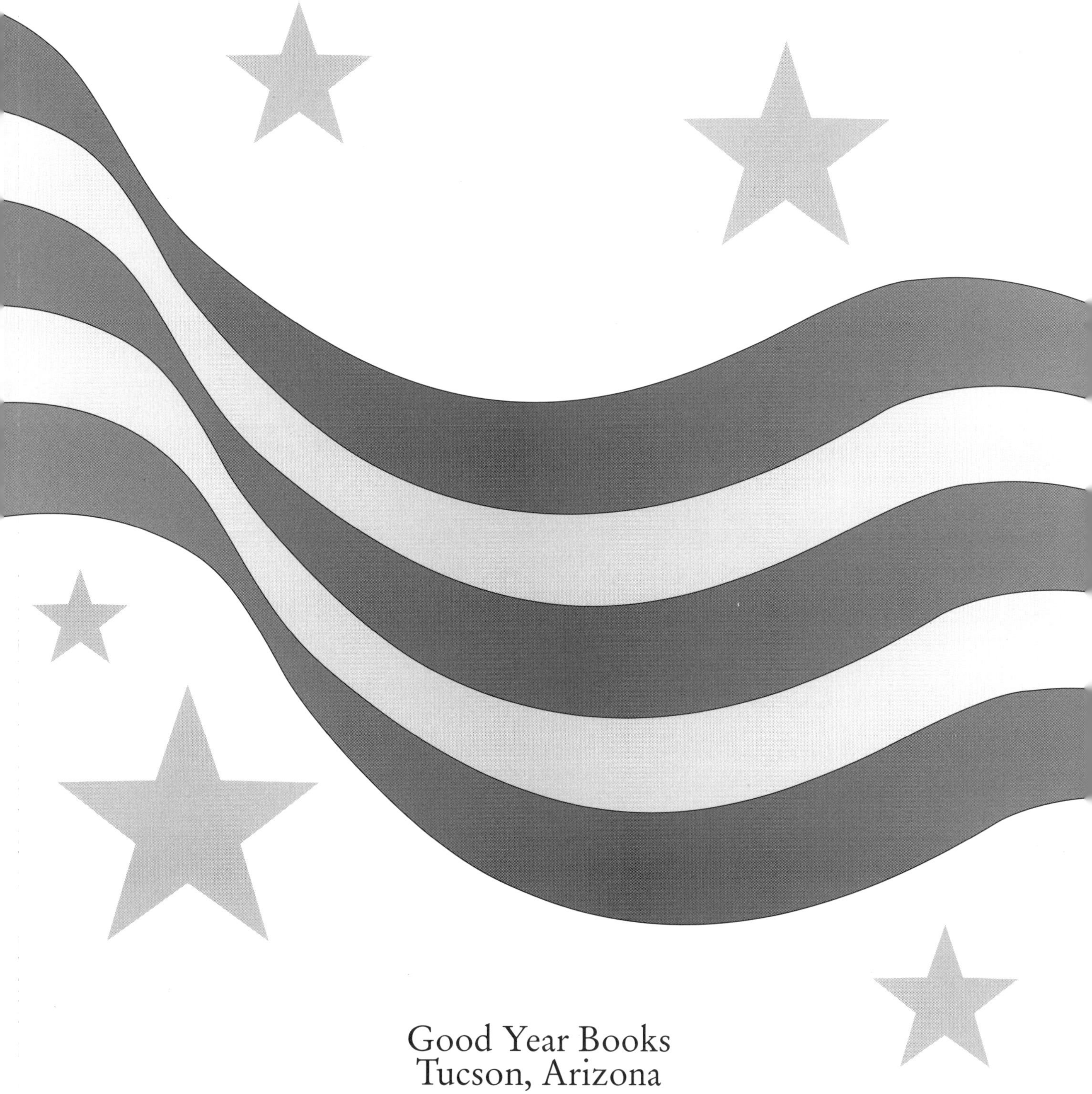

Good Year Books
Tucson, Arizona

Presidential Puzzlers

Dedicated
To Our Presidents
Past, Present, and Future

 **Good Year Books**

are available for most basic curriculum subjects plus many enrichment areas. For more Good Year Books, contact your local bookseller or educational dealer. For a complete catalog with information about other Good Year Books, please contact:

Good Year Books
P. O. Box 91858
Tucson, AZ 85752-1858
www.goodyearbooks.com

Book design and illustrations by Amy O'Brien Krupp.
Copyright © 1999, 2005 Good Year Books.
All Rights Reserved.
Printed in the United States of America.

ISBN-13 978-1-59647-048-4
ISBN-10 1-59647-048-8
Previous ISBN 0-673-58654-5

2 3 4 5 6 7 8 9 - ML - 09 08 07 06

Only portions of this book intended for classroom use may be reproduced without permission in writing from the publisher.

Presidential Puzzlers

Preface

The President of the United States is the most powerful person in the country and one of the most powerful in the world. Students need information about the men who have filled this position in order to understand the overwhelming responsibilities and problems, both at home and abroad, that have faced presidents through the years.

Each president arrived at this office from a different background and with a different personality and beliefs. Some rose from extreme poverty, others came from great wealth, but each had a burning desire to make a difference in this world and to help the America he loved and served.

The games in these pages cover each president's life from birth through retirement or death. Several presidents are still living.

Fairly short and simplified biographies of each man are available in libraries. Reading a biography to students can enhance their interest, inspire goals, and add to information found in textbooks.

Jeanne Cheyney and Arnold Cheyney

Contents

1. **George Washington** 1789–1797 1
2. **John Adams** 1797–1801 4
3. **Thomas Jefferson** 1801–1809 7
4. **James Madison** 1809–1817 10
5. **James Monroe** 1817–1825 13
6. **John Quincy Adams** 1825–1829 16
7. **Andrew Jackson** 1829–1837 19
8. **Martin Van Buren** 1837–1841 22
9. **William H. Harrison** 1841 25
10. **John Tyler** 1841–1845 28
11. **James K. Polk** 1845–1849 31
12. **Zachary Taylor** 1849–1850 34
13. **Millard Fillmore** 1850–1853 37
14. **Franklin Pierce** 1853–1857 40
15. **James Buchanan** 1857–1861 43
16. **Abraham Lincoln** 1861–1865 46
17. **Andrew Johnson** 1865–1869 49
18. **Ulysses S. Grant** 1869–1877 52
19. **Rutherford B. Hayes** 1877–1881 55
20. **James A. Garfield** 1881 58
21. **Chester A. Arthur** 1881–1885 61
22. **Grover Cleveland** 1885–1889 64
23. **Benjamin Harrison** 1889–1893 67
24. **Grover Cleveland** 1893–1897 70
25. **William McKinley** 1897–1901 73
26. **Theodore Roosevelt** 1901–1909 76
27. **William H. Taft** 1909–1913 79
28. **Woodrow Wilson** 1913–1921 82
29. **Warren G. Harding** 1921–1923 85
30. **Calvin Coolidge** 1923–1929 88
31. **Herbert C. Hoover** 1929–1933 91
32. **Franklin D. Roosevelt** 1933–1945 ... 94
33. **Harry S. Truman** 1945–1953 97
34. **Dwight D. Eisenhower** 1953–1961 ... 100
35. **John F. Kennedy** 1961–1963 103
36. **Lyndon B. Johnson** 1963–1969 106
37. **Richard M. Nixon** 1969–1974 109
38. **Gerald R. Ford** 1974–1977 112
39. **James E. Carter, Jr.** 1977–1981 115
40. **Ronald W. Reagan** 1981–1989 118
41. **George H. W. Bush** 1989–1993 121
42. **William J. Clinton** 1993–2001 124
43. **George W. Bush** 2001-2009 127

Answers 131

Suggested Reading 149

George Washington
1789–1797

CROSSWORD PUZZLE

ACROSS

2. George learned to plant and prepare _____ for market.
4. As a boy he explored the _____ around the plantation.
5. Favorite school subject: _____
8. When George was 11, his father _____.
9. He worked very _____. (diligently)
10. A plantation vegetable crop: _____
12. Wanted to join the British Royal Navy and be a _____; his mother said "no."
14. Father Augustine's first wife, _____, died.
15. Another plantation vegetable crop: _____
16. The Washingtons owned 20 _____.
17. George had a _____ throat before he died.
19. Favorite sport: _____ hunting (animal)
21. Liked _____ and fishing.
22. _____day: February 22, 1732
23. Favorite farm animal: _____
26. Mother's name: _____ (Augustine's second wife)
27. After Father died, George helped Mother manage their large farm called a _____.

DOWN

1. Liked rowing a BOAT on the river.
3. He had no _____ of his own. (heir)
5. Father's name: _____
6. When George joined the army, there were 13 _____.
7. George was Mary's Second child. (order)
9. After the war, George was a famous _____.
11. First job that earned him money: _____ (measuring land)
13. Watched sailing ships go by on the _____.
17. Augustine and Mary had _____ children. (number)
18. George went to school about _____ years.
19. He liked to catch _____ in the river.
20. Birth state: _____
21. Two school subjects: geography and _____ (the past)
24. A grain crop: _____
25. A vegetable and cattle-food crop: _____

George Washington
1789–1797

CROSSING OVER
DIRECTIONS
Use a pencil for this game. Find words from the following list that have the correct number of spaces and letters to fit into the crossing-over boxes (the words not in parentheses). Each word has a place where it belongs. The first word is done for you. To continue, find a nine-letter word having an "e" in the second space. All the words tell about George Washington.

3 letters
(1773) tea (thrown overboard at Boston)
(over) six (feet tall)

4 letters
Mary (George's mother)
(joined) army (at 21)
(Ferry Farm—family) home

5 letters
(colonies refused to pay) taxes (to England)
diary (kept by George)
Pope's (Creek Plantation, birthplace)
quiet (as a boy)
saved (his money)
(commander in) chief

6 letters
(1759: George married) Martha
(1778: starvation, misery at) Valley (Forge)
(Mount) Vernon (home)
horses (for farm, travel)

7 letters
(1775: a first war battle was) Concord
(Williamsburg, VA) capital
Potomac (R. flowed by Mount Vernon)
(great) courage (in battle)

8 letters
Virginia (home state)
expenses (kept records)
(liked brother) Lawrence
(had) schooner (for crops)

9 letters
(did) surveying
respected (his elders)
(he was) observant

10 letters
Cornwallis (surrendered)

11 letters
Continental (army ragged)

12 letters
Rappahannock (R. bordered Ferry Farm)

13 letters
Conotocarious (George's Indian name)

14 letters
Fredericksburg (near Ferry Farm)

George Washington
1789–1797

NAME A PLACE WHERE WASHINGTON AND TROOPS NEARLY STARVED AND FROZE

DIRECTIONS
Fill in the dotted lines with your answers. If they are correct, the circled letters will spell the place where Washington and troops nearly starved.

1. Wife's name: Martha
2. At Yorktown, British Lord Cornwallis surrendered with 8,000 troops.
3. Washington was the First president.
4. Since the Revolutionary War, George's _____ has been celebrated every February.
5. George's army officers wanted to make him _____. (monarch)
6. 1789: He was inaugurated as first _____.
7. Washington was called "the Father of his country."
8. One of the first battles of the war was fought at Concord
9. Some battles were lost; some were Won.
10. George fought in the French and Indian War.
11. He fought with the Continental Army. (name)
12. At 21, George Joined the army.

1. (M)artha
2. C(O)RNWALLIS
3. Fi(r)st
4. Bi(r)thday
5. K(i)ng
6. Pre(s)ident
7. Father
8. C(o)NCORD
9. (W)ON
10. Fre(n)ch
11. C(o)ntinental
12. (J)oined

SKYSCRAPER

DIRECTIONS
Write your answers in the boxes. The circled letters will help you.

1. George was over six feet tall.
2. Martha was short. (refers to height)
3. The Mount Vernon plantation covered 8,000 Acres of land.
4. Hogs were used to make bacon. (fried food)
5. A fruit grown on the farm: ~~Banana~~ Apples
6. Mount Vernon had its own men to lay _____. (building materials)
7. At 3:00 P.M., _____ was served.
8. Mount Vernon had its own _____. (grinder of grain)
9. Poultry animals: _____
10. Mount Vernon had its own _____ to shoe horses and make repairs.

1. Six
2. Short
3. Acres
4. Bac(O)n
5. Apples
6. B(R)icks
7. Dinner
8. M(I)ller
9. Chickens
10. Black(S)mith

John Adams
1797–1801

CROSSWORD PUZZLE

ACROSS

1. John's great, great grandfather, a Puritan, was _____ in his home country. (treated badly)
6. John was born _____, 30, 1735.
7. Farm animals: _____
9. Cattle and food crop: _____
11. His grandfather's name: _____ Adams
12. John was a _____; he loved his country.
13. He was very _____. (truthful)
14. He was not _____. (refers to weight)
19. He was _____. (refers to height)
21. John started school when he was _____. (age)
22. He knew how to _____ before he started school.
25. Garden crops: _____
26. 1758: He studied to become a _____. (profession)
28. _____: a favorite game of children (running game)
29. Winter: Boys and girls _____ on the ice.
30. Father, also named John, was a farmer and _____ maker. (for feet)
31. A favorite game: hop_____

DOWN

2. Mother's name: _____
3. Farm animals: _____
4. Father's first name: _____
5. John's birthplace: _____, MA
8. 1638: Great, great grandfather, Henry, came to America from _____.
10. A grain crop: _____
13. If the hearth fire went out, John got _____ coals from a neighbor.
15. He liked riding a _____. (animal)
16. In spring, boys liked _____-flying.
17. Boyhood chore: caring for _____, ducks, and geese
18. Favorite rough activity of boys: _____
20. A game played on the bare ground in spring: _____
21. Friendly Indians traded _____ and game for shoes John's father made.
23. John's home as a boy and man was near the _____ Ocean.
24. He helped his father with the _____ work.
27. Favorite boys' game, then: called rounders; now: _____ ball

John Adams
1797–1801

WORD SEARCHING
DIRECTIONS
In the grid, find these hidden words about John Adams (the words that are not in parentheses). They can go up, down, across, at an angle, forward, or backward.

(1754: he wanted) **freedom** (from England)

(1764: John married) **Abigail** (Smith)

(Abigail) **read** (many books)

(England ruled the 13) **colonies**

(1773: angry men threw English tea into the) **water**

(1765: England demanded taxes, and John was) **angry**

(John wrote newspaper articles about) **unfair** (taxes)

(John was a) **famous** (lawyer and patriot)

(1775: a first battle at) **Bunker** (Hill)

(John never joined the) **militia** (or fought)

(Abigail was very) **quiet**

(Abigail was also very) **wise**

(the Adamses had) **five** (children)

France (helped the colonies win the war against England)

(factories began producing) **wool** (cloth)

(1775: Congress formed the Continental) **Army**

(John signed the Declaration of) **Independence**

(John gave excellent) **speeches**

(1789: Washington was president; John was vice-) **president**

(1797: John became) **second** (president)

(John was the first president to live in what is now called the) **White** (House)

(John's) **son** (became president later)

1826: Thomas Jefferson and John) **died** (on the same day)

(mother's name:) **Susanna**

A	N	O	Y	M	R	A	S	T	B	V	W	S
B	P	R	E	A	D	N	U	M	U	S	P	U
I	S	E	I	N	O	L	O	C	N	L	R	S
G	A	C	F	G	D	H	M	J	K	M	E	A
A	R	B	S	R	V	W	A	T	E	R	S	N
I	Z	I	A	Y	C	G	F	D	R	H	I	N
L	B	N	L	S	P	Q	R	T	V	S	D	A
W	Y	D	A	E	Z	C	X	E	D	I	E	D
S	P	E	E	C	H	E	S	J	K	D	N	G
F	M	P	L	O	P	T	O	W	H	I	T	E
R	U	E	Q	N	C	D	N	F	J	L	E	A
Y	U	N	X	D	E	H	K	G	E	V	I	F
V	N	D	Z	M	I	O	R	P	N	T	U	R
T	F	E	Y	U	A	X	E	S	I	W	Q	A
E	A	N	V	D	W	O	O	L	W	B	C	N
S	I	C	F	I	H	K	I	Q	L	Z	J	C
F	R	E	E	D	O	M	P	O	R	M	N	E

John Adams
1797–1801

NUMBER CODE
DIRECTIONS
Look at the numbers under each line. Find the matching numbers in the code box, and write the letters on the corresponding answer lines.

1. In 1770, John was famous for D E F E N D I N G British soldiers in the Boston Massacre.

2. In 1797, John was I N A U G U R A T E D president.

3. 1800: John and Abigail M O V E D into the president's M A N S I O N.

4. The president's mansion (later called the White House) was not F I N I S H E D in any R O O M when they M O V E D in.

5. Abigail H U N G her W A S H I N G in the East R O O M.

6. John convinced Congress to form the C O N T I N E N T A L Army.

7. B O S T O N was the largest town in the colonies.

A - 1	N - 14
B - 2	O - 15
C - 3	P - 16
D - 4	Q - 17
E - 5	R - 18
F - 6	S - 19
G - 7	T - 20
H - 8	U - 21
I - 9	V - 22
J - 10	W - 23
K - 11	X - 24
L - 12	Y - 25
M - 13	Z - 26

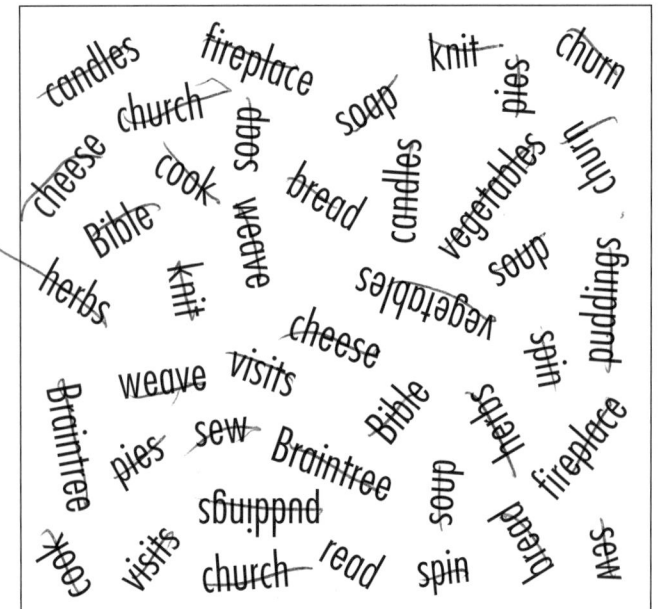

JOHN AND ABIGAIL ADAMS HOME PAIRS
DIRECTIONS
All of the words in the square tell about John and Abigail Adams' home. Each word is written twice except for one. Write the name of each pair on a line. (Cross off the pairs as you find them.) Then find the word that appears only once and write it in the box.

- Bible
- Church
- Churn
- Soap
- Braintree
- knit
- candles
- cheese
- pies
- fireplace
- sew
- soup
- herbs
- vegetables
- cook
- puddings
- visits
- spin
- bread
- weave

READ

Thomas Jefferson
1801–1809

CROSSWORD PUZZLE

ACROSS

3. 1801: Jefferson was the _____ president. (number)
4. The family owned _____ who worked for them.
7. Thomas admired Patrick Henry's _____. (talks)
10. Born: _____ 13, 1743
11. He had _____ hair and freckles. (color)
12. He often studied _____ hours a day. (number)
14. When Thomas was 14, his father _____.
15. He was over _____ feet tall.
16. He studied _____ to become a lawyer. (subject)
19. Patrick _____ gave fiery speeches against England.
20. Thomas played the _____ very well. (musical instrument)
21. He called his house and land _____.
22. 1772: Thomas married _____ Skelton.
23. Birthplace, Shadwell Plantation, grew much _____.
24. He loved _____ through forests.
25. Father's occupation: _____
27. Thomas and Martha played _____ together. (music term)
28. England, to pay its own war _____, taxed the colonies.

DOWN

1. Home state: _____
2. Mother's name: _____
5. Thomas studied at a boarding _____.
6. Father's plantation was called _____.
8. Father's name: _____
9. Martha loved playing the _____. (musical instrument)
13. Had _____ brothers and sisters.
14. Hunted _____ in the mountains.
17. 1760: He went to William and Mary College in _____, VA.
18. Thomas wrote the first draft of the Declaration of _____.
21. The name of Thomas's house and land means "little _____."
26. Martha and Thomas had five daughters and _____ son.

Thomas Jefferson
1801–1809

SUPPLY THE VOWEL
DIRECTIONS
In the grid, look for the following words (the words that are not in parentheses). The words can go up, down, across, at angles, backward, or forward. Parts of words may overlap. Supply the correct vowel—a e i o u—for the center of each word group.

Shadwell (name of childhood plantation)

(at Shadwell) **water** (wheel for grinding grain)

slaves

tobacco (crop)

(hunted) **deer**

(hunted) **squirrels**

(hunted wild) **turkeys**

bears (in the woods)

wolves (reward for)

Tuckahoe (Plantation was also his childhood home)

peach (trees)

soap (making)

smoke (houses for curing meat)

(small) **private** (school)

(teacher) **hired**

(learned) **arithmetic**

(learned to) **read**

(learned to) **write**

(goose) **quill** (pens)

ink

A	S	C	B	F	H	M	R	J	S	T	W	K
I	T	L	E	W	P	X	W	E	K	O	M	S
V	S	H	O	D	W	E	L	L	L	B	A	Y
G	A	T	R	V	L	Q	Z	V	H	A	I	P
O	E	A	S	U	E	D	E	P	L	C	F	N
R	J	R	C	L	T	S	C	L	R	C	K	Q
S	M	I	U	N	T	Q	I	L	R	O	K	Q
G	V	T	B	W	T	O	R	K	E	Y	S	Y
S	D	H	F	R	Q	I	C	O	M	P	K	E
G	P	M	E	I	L	R	S	K	R	H	Q	N
J	R	M	A	D	O	R	T	Y	A	X	W	E
V	D	T	A	Z	U	E	A	D	O	H	T	H
B	C	I	G	C	N	L	M	E	I	A	O	K
R	X	C	F	W	H	S	V	T	V	P	J	E
L	Y	D	H	C	K	J	H	I	R	E	D	Q
S	A	I	E	T	O	S	R	R	N	T	G	B
E	Z	N	P	W	U	P	Q	W	M	K	F	L

8

Thomas Jefferson
1801–1809

SAME FIRST LETTER
DIRECTIONS
Find two words that begin with the same letter for each of these letters. The circled letter is the first letter for each answer.

Example:

(R)   **R** E D — color of his hair
     R **I V E R** — where ships sailed

(M)   M _ _ _ _ _ — a daughter
     M _ _ _ _ _ — a daughter

(T)   T _ _ _ _ _ — soft red vegetable he grew
     T _ _ _ _ _ — a wild fowl

(S)   S _ _ _ _ _ _ _ — plantation (born there)
     S _ _ _ — something made for washing

(L)   L _ _ _ _ _ — occupation
     L _ _ _ — He owned lots of it.

(P)   P _ _ _ — something made from a goose quill
     P _ _ _ _ _ _ _ — daring men from Tripoli who attacked ships

(S)   S _ _ _ _ _ _ — his father's occupation
     S _ _ _ _ _ — people who worked on plantations

(A)   A _ _ _ _ — Jefferson's birth month
     A _ _ _ _ — a fruit Jefferson grew

(M)   M _ _ _ _ _ _ _ _ _ — name of his home and land
     M a r t h a — wife's name

CLUE
DIRECTIONS
Each set of lines has vowels and an occasional consonant to help you determine the correct answer. All the words tell about Thomas Jefferson.

1. Shadwell farm had these animals: _ o _ _ e _ , _ a _ _ _ e, _ o _ _
2. Thomas had a pet   m o _ _ i _ g _ i _ _ _   that sat on his shoulder.
3. At the farm, _ a _ was boiled and made into _ o a _ .
4. Meat was smoked and cured in a _ _ o _ e _ o u _ e.
5. Tuckahoe Plantation had a _ _ _ _ e and _ e a _ _ _ fruit trees growing.

James Madison
1809–1817

CROSSWORD PUZZLE

ACROSS

1. Madison's parents had _____ children.
7. As a child, he played with _____ children at the plantation. (bondage)
9. James was called the "_____ of the Constitution."
12. James wrote a plan for a strong central gov't: Congress makes laws; president leads; Supreme _____ interprets laws.
14. Birth state: _____
15. The plans he wrote for a strong gov't were called the _____.
17. Montpelier Plantation had 4,000 _____.
19. Madison and Jefferson wanted to be _____ from England.
21. James and his father had the _____ name.
23. Dolley's parents: plain people called _____.
25. At _____ 11, James went away to school.
26. In 1794, he married _____ Payne Todd, a widow.

DOWN

2. At 43, unmarried James Madison wanted a _____.
3. As the oldest son, James inherited his father's home and _____.
4. Mother's name: _____
5. Madison: a friend of Thomas _____
6. He was taught by a private _____.
7. Madison stated: When central government is weak and states are too _____, the country fails.
8. He always dressed in _____ clothes. (color)
10. 1775: Elected to represent his county at Virginia's capital, _____.
11. People of the states wanted a Bill of _____ added to the Constitution.
13. Name of father's plantation: _____
16. James suggested this title for the country's leader: "The President of the United _____."
18. After the Revolutionary War, Dolley's father gave his slaves their _____. (liberty)
20. Seven of James's siblings _____.
22. Madison persuaded Congress to make a law to feed Washington's starving _____.
24. As a child, he was not strong and was often _____.

10

James Madison
1809–1817

CROSSING OVER

DIRECTIONS

Use a pencil for this game. Using the words that are not in parentheses, find words from the following list that have the correct number of spaces and letters to fit into the crossing-over boxes. Each word has a place where it belongs. The first word is done for you. To continue, find an eight-letter word having an "h" in the second space. All the words tell about James Madison.

4 letters
- (Dolley had two) ~~sons~~
- (James loved to) ~~read~~
- (1790: Dolley had married John) ~~Todd~~

5 letters
- (Helped) ~~freed~~ (slaves go to Africa)
- (1793: Dolley became a) ~~widow~~
- (Madison: born) ~~March~~ (1751)
- (James: a) ~~small~~ (man)
- (Father's name:) ~~James~~
- (Dolley's first son:) ~~Payne~~ (Todd)
- (many died of yellow) ~~fever~~
- (Quaker dress was) ~~plain~~

6 letters
- (1809: Madison was elected) ~~fourth~~ (president)
- (Dolley helped her) ~~mother~~
- (1794: Madison married) ~~Dolley~~
- (1814: British) ~~burned~~ (most of Washington, D.C.)
- (Dolley's first husband) ~~lawyer~~

7 letters
- (Dolley: good) ~~hostess~~
- (Paynes and John Todd:) ~~Quakers~~
- (Dolley's second son) ~~William~~
- (1813: Lake Erie) ~~Admiral~~ (Perry's victory)
- (1814: president's) ~~mansion~~ (burned by British)

8 letters
- Virginia (Dolley's home state)
- (England) ~~captured~~ (U.S. ships' crews)
- (1814: Dolley saved) ~~painting~~ (of Washington from fire)
- (1817:) ~~Madisons~~ (given farewell honors)
- (he had four) ~~thousand~~ (books)

9 letters
- (James: Jefferson's) ~~secretary~~ (of state)
- (James helped get) ~~Louisiana~~ (Purchase)

10 letters
- (the Madisons' home) ~~Montpelier~~

12 letters
- (1783: Dolley Payne's family moved to) ~~Philadelphia~~
- (Dolley loved) ~~entertaining~~

James Madison
1809–1817

NAME HER HOME PLANTATION
DIRECTIONS
Fill in the dotted lines with your answers. If they are correct, the circled letters will spell the name of Dolley Madison's home plantation.

1. Fine ladies were dressed in satin and _____.
2. Most of the fine homes were built with _____. (building material)
3. Gentlemen rode on fine _____.
4. One of Dolley's childhood jobs was to scrub her home's front _____.
5. Washington, D.C., was a little town, with building construction, pigs in puddles, and goats and _____ grazing along streets.
6. 1783: The most important city in the colonies was the capital, _____, PA.
7. Dolley was a very _____ young woman. (looks)
8. _____ Burr brought James Madison to meet the young widow, Dolley.
9. Dolley, Washington's picture, and the original Declaration of Independence, escaped the burning city in _____. (vehicles)
10. Dolley started the tradition of egg _____ on the White House lawn at Easter.
11. A peace treaty with England was signed, and the war was _____.
12. Dolley served her guests a dessert called ice _____.

SCRAMBLED WORDS
DIRECTIONS
Unscramble the words and write the answers on the lines provided. Use scrap paper to work out your answers.

1. Dolley escaped the burning city of Washington, D.C., and carried these things to safety:

    velvet PRDASE _____

    OLCCK _____

    VILSRE _____

    George Washington's ATOPRRIT _____

    The GILORIAN Declaration of Independence and valuable records _____

2. Dolley and her black maid were dressed like MAFRSRE to fool the enemy. _____

3. Dolley and James were RUBEID at Montpelier. _____

James Monroe
1817–1825

CROSSWORD PUZZLE

ACROSS

3. 1773: Angry people in _____ refused to pay taxes. (city)
5. 1775: James and friends captured _____ and military supplies. (weapons)
7. _____ tax stamps: needed for buying and selling goods. (country)
8. James liked to shoot; often went _____.
9. He always treated others _____.
10. Was known as _____-working. (diligent)
12. He was a _____ child. (soft-spoken)
13. Washington called colonists _____, not British citizens.
15. Daughter _____ was born.
17. Mother and wife: both named _____.
20. Colonists were told they would be _____ for not buying tax stamps.
21. James and classmates practiced military _____. (routines)
22. 1774: Men from the _____ met in Philadelphia for a Continental Congress.

DOWN

1. 1775: England was _____ and sent ships to block Boston harbor.
2. James remained a _____ to sister, Elizabeth.
4. At 11, James walked to _____ each day.
6. Spence _____ a petition against the Stamp Act.
9. Men began _____ pamphlets and news articles.
11. Mother taught her children _____.
14. Father's name: _____.
16. 1766: The British decided to _____ the Stamp Act.
18. Spence owned five _____ acres of land.
19. 1765: Colonists refused to _____ British goods.

13

James Monroe
1817–1825

WORD SEARCHING
DIRECTIONS
In the grid, find these words about James Monroe (the words that are not in parentheses). The words can go up, down, across, at an angle, forward, or backward.

(mother taught James to) **read**
(1776: enlisted in Third Virginia) **Regiment**
(fought with Washington at) **Trenton** (N.J.)
(for wisdom and bravery; was promoted to Lt.) **Colonel**
(became a) **lawyer**
(1783: elected to) **Congress**
(traveled to Western) **Territory**
(1786) **married** (Elizabeth Kortright)
(1786: daughter) **Eliza** (born)
(in U.S.) **Senate**
(James and family in) **France**
(elected) **governor** (of Virginia)
Louisiana (Territory bought)
(1817: inaugurated) **fifth** (pres.)
(social affairs at the President's House were kept) **simple**
(construction of) **Erie** (Canal began)
(1819: first) **steamship** (crossed ocean)
(1820: Eliza married in President's) **House**
(1821: South American countries all) **independent**
(1823: Monroe) **Doctrine** (given to Congress in a speech)
(James Monroe's home:) **Oak** (Hill, Virginia)
(1831: Monroe) **died** (at age 73)

A	P	I	H	S	M	A	E	T	S	W	B	E
S	C	D	F	H	K	C	O	N	J	Q	C	T
Y	S	A	L	E	N	G	R	A	Z	I	L	E
N	F	E	P	A	E	G	L	M	H	P	M	R
R	N	R	R	U	T	P	L	A	W	Y	E	R
Y	E	F	D	G	A	E	P	R	O	F	S	I
I	B	G	M	V	N	W	C	R	I	T	H	T
N	O	R	I	O	E	O	D	I	E	D	L	O
D	M	L	L	M	S	R	C	E	U	B	N	R
E	N	O	T	N	E	R	T	D	E	D	V	Y
P	C	U	W	R	O	N	R	E	V	O	G	W
E	B	I	T	A	E	S	T	G	A	C	C	A
N	F	S	J	G	L	M	A	K	C	T	I	H
D	I	I	V	H	P	U	D	E	J	R	V	O
E	F	A	B	S	M	I	K	I	D	I	Y	U
N	T	N	E	D	I	S	E	R	P	N	E	S
T	H	A	L	W	S	K	A	E	Y	E	K	E

14

James Monroe
1817–1825

BOYHOOD FARM PAIRS
DIRECTIONS
All the words in the large box tell about something that was found on James Monroe's boyhood farm. Each word is written twice, except for one. Write the name of each pair on a line. (Cross off the pairs as you find them.) Then find the name that appears only once and write it in the box.

Pigs — cows
pillows — mattresses
rifles — parsnips
quilts — butter
tables — milk
chairs — eggs
chickens — squash
geese — turnips
cabinets — cheese
chests — horses
potatoes — tools

GUNPOWDER

MONROE DOCTRINE NUMBER CODE
DIRECTIONS
Look at the numbers under each line. Find the matching numbers in the code box, and write the letters on the corresponding answer lines.

In 1822, Pres. Monroe recognized S. American countries as **R E P U B L I C S**.
18 5 16 21 2 12 9 3 19

In 1823, the Monroe Doctrine was given in speech to **C O N G R E S S**.
3 15 14 7 18 5 19 19

The Monroe Doctrine states:

1. Western nations are Republics, not **M O N A R C H I E S**.
13 15 14 1 18 3 8 9 5 19

2. Western nations are not subject to **F U T U R E** colonization.
6 21 20 21 18 5

3. The U.S. would protect the Western Hemisphere from hostile **I N T E N T**.
9 14 20 5 14 20

4. The U.S. would not interfere in **W A R S** inside European countries.
23 1 18 19

A - 1	N - 14
B - 2	O - 15
C - 3	P - 16
D - 4	Q - 17
E - 5	R - 18
F - 6	S - 19
G - 7	T - 20
H - 8	U - 21
I - 9	V - 22
J - 10	W - 23
K - 11	X - 24
L - 12	Y - 25
M - 13	Z - 26

John Quincy Adams
1825–1829

CROSSWORD PUZZLE

ACROSS

2. Colonists were angry about the British _____ Act.
3. He rode a _____ to and from Boston with mail.
4. Wrote short articles and became _____. (well-known)
6. Birthplace: _____, MA
9. 1775: Saw a war battle from his _____.
11. John helped his mother with the farm while his father was at the Continental _____ in Philadelphia.
14. 1775: Militiamen on _____ Hill fought the British.
15. Louisa: wife's _____
16. Winter: John took a _____ pan to bed.
17. His father had been the _____ U.S. president.
19. At 14, John was secretary for an envoy to St. Petersburg, _____. (country)
20. 1819: John signed a treaty with _____; U.S. bought Florida.
21. British "_____coats" made sure tax laws were obeyed.
22. British soldiers marched to the rhythm of fifes and _____.

DOWN

1. The Adamses: _____ sons, one daughter
2. 1803: Elected to the U.S. _____.
4. On a ship to France, John learned to speak _____. (language)
5. 1802: Was elected to _____ Senate.
7. John and his father went to the _____; John skated on frozen canals. (country)
8. John had _____ getting along with people. (difficulty)
10. Tried to make the U.S. _____ and respected. (mighty)
11. Went to France on a ship with heavy _____ for protection.
12. Mother's name: _____
13. Letters were folded and _____ with wax.
18. Wrote in his _____ daily.
19. Mother taught John to _____ and write.

John Quincy Adams
1825–1829

SUPPLY THE VOWEL

DIRECTIONS
In the grid, look for the following words (the words that are not in parentheses). The words can go up, down, across, at angles, backward, or forward. Parts of words may overlap. Supply the correct vowel—a e i o u—for the center of each word group.

(Pres. Washington sent John to the Netherlands as) **minister**

(1797: John married) **Louisa** (in London)

(her mother was) **British**

(her father was) **American**

(she) **grew** (up in England)

(John was elected to the Massachusetts State) **Senate**

(1803: Washington, D.C., had one) **street** (——Pennsylvania Avenue)

(Pennsylvania Avenue was) **mud** (and dirt)

E	B	I	H	U	A	Q	D	S	M	C	E	X
V	N	R	J	S	B	R	I	T	○	S	H	O
Y	S	G	M	E	D	L	P	T	N	X	N	W
A	T	C	L	N	W	V	Y	R	I	Y	T	G
Y	I	S	T	○	T	E	K	Z	S	D	F	H
G	B	E	R	T	N	A	S	W	T	F	U	F
T	F	S	C	E	G	D	A	H	E	J	S	W
C	R	S	M	N	C	J	I	M	R	Q	F	G
L	O	○	I	S	A	C	L	S	L	K	I	K
R	D	C	S	I	F	L	○	R	I	D	A	L
E	M	S	V	S	H	N	R	W	L	P	S	U
T	A	I	B	N	I	H	S	G	S	T	V	W
M	O	D	U	W	Z	A	P	Q	R	E	E	Q
C	I	P	G	S	N	A	C	I	R	○	M	A
M	V	U	E	J	D	K	Y	O	D	R	W	B
R	Y	J	N	W	N	P	B	S	O	T	D	T
Q	C	A	D	O	B	F	S	H	L	S	T	K

(In Washington, D.C.,) **cows**, (pigs, and geese wandered around loose)

(Washington, D.C.:) **weeds** (grew in park areas)

(Washington, D.C., was called a wilderness) **city**

(John and Pres. Jefferson liked to) **discuss** (many things)

(when John got to) **Russia** (he learned to speak Russian)

(England continued kidnapping American) **sailors**

(In 1812) **war** (was declared on England)

(John was sent as minister to) **England**

(1816: Pres. Madison made John secretary of) **state**

(John and Spanish ambassador signed treaty that gave U.S.) **Florida** (for $5,000,000)

(In 1825, John was elected) **sixth** (president)

(John was the only president who was the) **son** (of a former president)

17

John Quincy Adams
1825–1829

CLUE
DIRECTIONS

Each set of lines has vowels and an occasional consonant to help you determine the correct answer. All the words tell about John Quincy Adams.

1. Before wife Louisa was 5, she spoke English and __ __ e __ c __ fluently.
2. When Louisa was 20, she met __ o __ __.
3. 1797: John and Louisa were __ a __ r i e __.
4. Louisa met Empress Elizabeth and also met Alexander I, who was the __ __ a __ of Russia.
5. The fashionable ladies at the court of Alexander I wore rich furs, beautiful gowns, and sparkling __ e __ e __ __.
6. John became secretary of __ __ a __ e in Washington.
7. 1825: John finally became the U.S. __ __ e __ i __ e __ __.
8. In summer, Pres. Adams rose early and swam in the __ o __ o __ a __ R.
9. After swimming, John returned to the President's House and read his __ i __ l e.
10. Many of the o a __ trees around the White House today were planted by John.
11. John used his influence in establishing the famous museum in Washington, D.C., the __ __ i __ __ s o __ i a __ Institution.

WORDS IN WORDS
DIRECTIONS

John Quincy Adams was born in a house in Braintree, Massachusetts (now called Quincy). Next to the house is a nearly identical house where his father, John, was born. How many words can you make from the letters in "nearly identical houses"?

Andrew Jackson
1829–1837

CROSSWORD PUZZLE

ACROSS

1. 1775: Andrew was _____ years old.
4. 1759: Andy's brother came to America, with the British, to fight _____.
5. Andy had great _____ and intelligence.
7. He was the _____ president. (number)
10. Had a brother, _____, born in Ireland
11. Andy's nickname was "Old _____."
12. At 5: Known as a spunky _____. (using fists)
14. Wanted a prized Barlow _____. (whittling tool)
15. Father died of a _____ attack before Andy's birth.
16. Andy: full of _____ (pep)
19. Spent much time with his bow and _____.
21. At 6, he got a pop_____ and pretended to hunt.
22. Andrew read newspapers to people not able to _____.
23. 1781: Andy was captured; when he refused to clean a British officer's _____, the officer slashed him.
24. Mrs. Jackson helped her sister, _____.
25. Andrew: _____ six days after father's death.
26. 1765: Andy's Irish parents landed by ship at _____, PA.

DOWN

2. Andy's other brother, _____, born in Ireland.
3. Andy was named _____, for his father.
4. Parents came from _____. (country)
5. Andrew was devoted to his _____. (land where he lived)
6. People said Andrew was as _____ as hickory wood.
8. Mother's sisters lived in South _____. (state)
9. Andrew's family was _____. (little money)
13. Andrew was very _____ and learned well. (smart)
15. Father bought a wagon and _____ to travel from Philadelphia to SC. (animals)
17. Mother's name: _____
18. At 13, Andy _____ in the militia.
20. Elizabeth had four _____ in America. (siblings)
25. Hugh, at 9, made Andy a _____ and arrows.

Andrew Jackson
1829–1837

CROSSING OVER

DIRECTIONS

Use a pencil for this game. Using the words that are not in parentheses, find words from the following list that have the correct number of spaces and letters to fit into the crossing-over boxes. Each word has a place where it belongs. The first word is done for you. To continue, find a nine-letter word with an "s" in the fourth space. All the words tell about Andrew Jackson.

3 letters
(due to) **war** (good prices for cattle)
(His mother said, "Never) **lie**(.")
(he studied) **law**
(determined, strong-willed) **man**

4 letters
(1781: his mother) **died**
(1815: was Major Gen. in) **army**
(Jackson) **thin**
(Jackson demanded) **same** (pay for blacks as other soldiers)

5 letters
(born) **March** (1767)
(as a boy, used a) **rifle**
(went on a cattle) **drive** (to Charles Town, SC)
(British took seamen from U.S. ships by) **force**
(Jackson's shabby uniform:) **faded** (blue color, buckskin, unpolished boots)

6 letters
(in Jackson's army were freed) **blacks**
(boyhood home) **Waxhaw** (SC)
(brother Hugh:) **killed** (in battle)
(1797: was in U.S.) **Senate**
(His mother said, "Be) **honest**(.")
(he became a) **lawyer**
(taught) **school** (for a while)

7 letters
(in Jackson's army were) **Indians**
(in Jackson's army were) **pirates**
(defended children) **smaller** (than himself)
(British captured) **Charles** (Town)
(Andy was maj.) **general** (in the army)
(became gov. of) **Florida**

8 letters
soldiers (loved their leader)
(Jackson built) **ramparts** (of earth)

9 letters
(was first) **Tennessee** (member of the U.S. House of Representatives)
(1828: became seventh) **president**

10 letters
(in Jackson's army were) **militiamen**

11 letters
(had few) **experienced** (soldiers)

12 letters
(in Jackson's army were) **backwoodsmen**

Andrew Jackson
1829–1837

NAME THE PLACE WHERE ANDREW JACKSON STUDIED LAW

DIRECTIONS

Fill in the dotted lines with your answers. If they are correct, the circled letters will spell the name of the place where Andrew Jackson studied law.

1. Andrew's mother, Mrs. _____, died when he was 14, making him an orphan.
2. At 17, Jackson studied to be a _____. (profession)
3. He studied hard for his chosen profession in North _____. (state)
4. At 21, Andrew moved to a frontier town in TN called _____. (now a city)
5. Andrew handled about half the court _____ in his area of TN.
6. Jackson _____ 650 acres of land for a plantation and mansion.
7. For six years, Jackson was a _____ in Superior Court. (made decisions)
8. Andrew married _____ Donelson.
9. Andrew and Rachel were _____ living in their mansion, the Hermitage, in TN. (joyful)
10. Abbr. for the state where he studied law: _____
11. Birthplace: Waxhaw, South _____

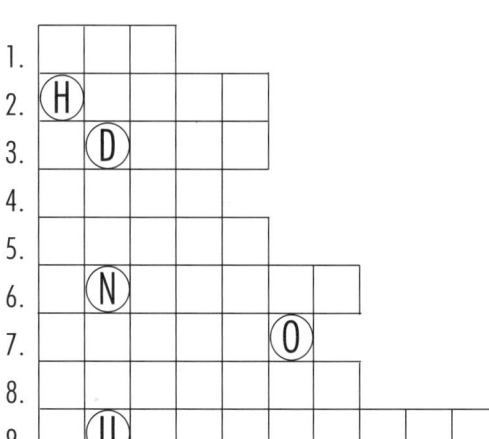

SKYSCRAPER

DIRECTIONS

Write your answers in the boxes. The circled letters will help you.

1. Jackson was called "_____ Hickory."
2. 1828: The mansion where President Jackson lived in Washington was called the President's _____.
3. In 1824, John Quincy _____ won the presidency, not Andrew Jackson.
4. 1828: Rachel _____ of a heart attack before Andy's inauguration.
5. After the inauguration, Jackson rode his _____ to the President's House.
6. During Jackson's term in office, the _____ were forced to move to western land against their will.
7. Andrew failed to buy Texas from _____.
8. The problem of _____ threatened to divide the U.S. (bondage)
9. 1845: Andrew died of _____. (a lung disease)

21

Martin Van Buren
1837–1841

CROSSWORD PUZZLE

ACROSS

6. 1796: At 14, he was an _____ to a lawyer.
8. Father's name: _____
9. Martin, 29, was elected State _____ for NY.
11. Martin and Hannah had four _____.
12. Martin's birthplace was _____, NY.
14. Slavery was _____-lawed in NY.
18. Mother's name: _____
19. He moved to _____ York City.
22. Van Buren family: _____ Dutch to each other, but English to customers.
24. 1819: After their youngest son was _____, Hannah died.
25. Fulton's new steamboat traveled up and down the _____ River.

DOWN

1. Born: _____, 1782
2. _____ coach travelers stopped at Van Burens' house.
3. Had _____ brothers and sisters.
4. 1812: Was in favor of _____ against England.
5. Martin got a bill passed ending debtors' _____. (places of confinement)
7. Lawyer Van Buren defended people who were _____ or rich, if they were wronged.
10. Martin, brothers, and sisters helped with house and farm _____.
11. 1807: first voyage of Fulton's _____ boat.
13. Ancestry: from the _____ (country)
15. Martin wrote: We are "the only _____ people on earth." (at liberty)
16. 1803: Martin became a _____. (profession)
17. As a boy, he seldom went to _____; he had too much work to do at home.
20. Martin liked to _____ to important government lawyers.
21. Hannah was _____. (ancestry)
23. He was born at the _____ of the Revolutionary War. (close)

Martin Van Buren
1837–1841

WORD SEARCHING
DIRECTIONS
In the grid, find these words about Martin Van Buren (the words that are not in parentheses). They can go up, down, across, at an angle, forward, or backward.

```
L A G E L A D I G J C L J
E S R E G N E S S A P F U
C M I N Q S O H B C D B T
Y L R X F S H R G K W Y B
A I O C P T P E W S O A Z
R P N T L E K P E O V C I
Q K R U H A M U N N S L K
M S F A R M T B C T X E V
A J Z D Q V R L S W N R K
E P T Y U X A I E C O M R
R Z M S F I L C H B G O Q
T M E A E A D A L B A N Y
S C N D R P G N O L R T W
P E U E I T R S M S A J N
U F D I F E I W X Y P Q T
G E V B H O H N J A F G Z
F N K D O W N S T R E A M
```

(political parties:) **Federalists** (for strong central gov't)

(Democratic-)**Republicans** (for citizens running the gov't)

(at 14, in the law office he) **swept** (the floor)

(kept stove) **fire** (burning)

(copied) **legal** (papers)

Martin (was a Democratic-Republican)

(1807) **steam**(ships carried:)
passengers
cloth
iron (products)
farm (products)

(stagecoach route from) **Albany** (to New York City)

(1812: 12,000) **men** (drafted in NY for war)

(1814:) **Jackson** (defeated the British at New Orleans)

(steamships went) **upstream** (and) **downstream**

(Fulton's first steamship:) *Clermont*

(Fulton's larger steamship:) *Paragon*

Martin Van Buren
1837–1841

MARTIN'S PRESIDENCY PAIRS
DIRECTIONS
All of the words in the large box relate to Martin Van Buren's presidency. Each word is written twice, except for one. Write the name of each pair on a line. (Cross off the pairs as you find them.) Then find the word that appears only once and write it in the box.

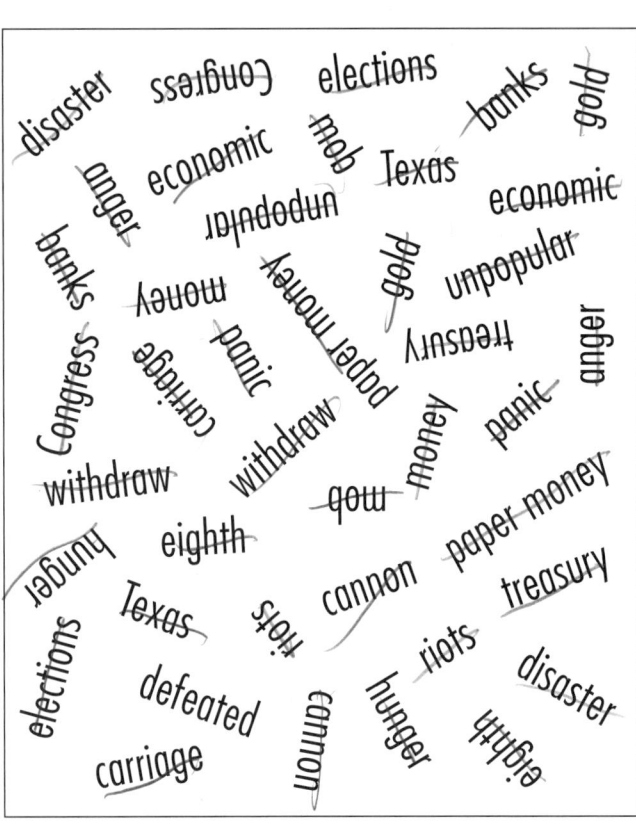

Texas / Congress
elections / gold
economic / anger
unpopular / withdraw
treasury / cannon
paper money / eighth
disaster / mob
money / carriage
panic / hunger
riots / banks

DEFEATED

SCRAMBLED WORDS
DIRECTIONS
Unscramble the words and write the answers on the lines provided. (Use scrap paper to work out your answers.)

1. President Jackson was elected for a EOSCDN term; and Van Buren was vice president. _____
2. Martin became the TIHEGH president. _____
3. Jackson was against the huge NABK of the United States. He believed that it benefited only the wealthy and big business. _____
4. Money was removed from the government bank and was not invested YWSILE. _____
5. The YCNEOOM collapsed. _____
6. People became poor and URHGYN. _____
7. Martin Van Buren was not LEREECTD. _____

24

William H. Harrison
1841

CROSSWORD PUZZLE

ACROSS

2. George _____ visited Berkeley, William's birthplace. (former pres.)
4. William wanted to be a _____. (medical profession)
6. George Washington had once held baby William on his _____.
7. William's army strategy won a victory at the Great Miami _____ in Ohio.
8. Pres. Washington made William an ensign in the _____.
11. Father took part in two Continental _____.
12. Father's name: _____
15. Harrison marched 80 new soldiers to Ft. _____. (now Pittsburgh)
16. Born: _____ 9, 1773
17. Harrison and troops rode on _____ boats down the Ohio R.
19. When he was 3, his father signed the _____ of Independence.
24. William, promoted to _____, led the command post at Ft. Washington, OH.
25. The _____ united against Gen. Wayne's forces.
26. Ft. Washington was near the _____ R.
27. William learned to hide in trees and shoot the _____.

DOWN

1. 1763: _____, the Ottawa Indian chief, tried to unite all tribes.
2. William fought under "Mad" Anthony _____, an excellent general.
3. As a child, he was taught at home by a _____.
5. Studied medicine at the University of _____ in Philadelphia. (state)
9. William asked Anna Symmes to marry him; she said, "_____."
10. He was the _____ child in the family. (rank)
13. Mother's name: _____
14. Birth state: _____
18. Benjamin _____ (statesman and inventor) visited Berkeley.
20. 1632: The first William Harrison who came to America was _____. (citizen of England)
21. William marched his troops to Ft. Pitt with a drummer's _____ keeping rhythm.
22. Lt. Meriwether _____ at Ft. Pitt.
23. Anna's father was a _____. (made court decisions)

William H. Harrison
1841

SUPPLY THE VOWEL

DIRECTIONS

In the grid, look for the following words (the words that are not in parentheses). The words can go up, down, across, at angles, backward, or forward. Parts of words may overlap. Supply the correct vowel—a e i o u—for the center of each word group.

- (he learned to slash) **trees** (for trails)
- (William) **Clark** (a Lt. at Fort Pitt)
- (early Northwest Territory states)
  Ohio (eastern part)
  Indiana
  Illinois
  MI (abbreviation for Michigan)
  Wisconsin
- (1791: Harrison's father) **died**
- (Harrison learned to fight like the) **enemy**
- (William was apprenticed to a) **doctor**
- (he learned how to use) **knives** (on the enemy)
- (a feared Indian leader) **Tecumseh**
- (Tecumseh wanted all tribes) **united** (to fight)
- (an Ohio Indian chief: Little) **Turtle**
- (Harrison was promoted to) **Captain** (at Ft. Washington)
- (his army won a victory at the Great) **Miami** (R. in Ohio)
- (Tecumseh was) **killed** (at the Battle of the Thames)
- (Harrison) **pursued** (the enemies and won victories)
- (William enlisted in the) **army**
- (Harrison's mansion in Indiana:) **Grouse** (land)

K	A	F	M	D	L	E	R	Y	T	D	B	S
W	O	S	C	O	N	S	I	N	M	I	E	N
M	N	L	V	S	A	K	N	I	V	O	S	U
G	D	H	L	Z	C	B	H	I	R	D	N	P
K	I	J	N	E	O	I	F	T	O	P	U	E
Y	A	G	Q	S	D	A	M	P	N	R	J	Q
D	N	C	Y	K	Q	L	T	O	S	Y	P	Z
M	A	L	R	E	T	E	C	U	M	S	E	H
H	J	I	E	R	D	G	E	N	R	W	A	K
W	G	L	W	B	K	D	N	I	E	T	I	V
C	Y	L	X	M	E	R	O	T	J	P	L	H
I	B	I	C	S	L	Y	S	E	I	U	R	E
F	K	N	U	F	W	T	M	D	C	F	I	S
M	D	O	C	T	O	R	E	R	L	M	B	T
P	R	I	H	V	C	A	P	T	A	I	N	A
G	E	S	C	I	H	U	L	I	R	U	V	Q
D	A	J	Z	N	O	G	M	P	K	D	M	T

26

William H. Harrison
1841

NAME THE FORT THAT WAS DIFFERENT IN ONE WAY

DIRECTIONS

Fill in the dotted lines with your answers. If they are correct, the circled letters will spell the name of the fort that was different in one way.

1. Harrison was given the rank of _____ at Ft. Washington in Ohio.
2. Gov. Harrison's mansion in Indiana was called _____.
3. Harrison's forces defeated the Indians at the Battle of _____. (a river)
4. The Indians made an ambush of fallen trees at the Battle of Fallen _____.
5. In 1799, the (Old) Northwest Territory was divided into two parts: Ohio on the east; and the second part, Indiana, Michigan, Illinois, and Wisconsin on the west, called _____ Territory.
6. Gen. Wayne circled the fighting Indians and _____ in on them.
7. _____ were in charge of this fort that was different from any other. (females)
8. During the War of 1812, Gov. Harrison had an _____ tunnel dug under his mansion in case of Indian attacks.
9. The Indians united under this feared leader: _____.

NUMBER CODE

DIRECTIONS

Look at the numbers under each line. Find the matching numbers in the code box, and write the letters on the corresponding answer lines.

1. Harrison was the N I N T H   P R E S I D E N T.
   14 9 14 20 8   16 18 5 19 9 4 5 14 20

2. He was I N A U G U R A T E D on M A R C H 4, 1841.
   9 14 1 21 7 21 18 1 20 5 4   13 1 18 3 8

3. At his March inauguration, he talked for T W O   H O U R S, the L O N G E S T
   20 23 15   8 15 21 18 19   12 15 14 7 5 19 20
   of any U.S. president before him.

4. Inauguration Day was C O L D and W E T.
   3 15 12 4   23 5 20

5. His W I F E W A S I L L A T T H E I R
   23 9 6 5 23 1 19 9 12 12 1 20 20 8 5 9 18
   H O M E U P N O R T H and didn't attend the inauguration.
   8 15 13 5 21 16 14 15 18 20 8

6. Harrison C A U G H T A C O L D.
   3 1 21 7 8 20 1 3 15 12 4

7. By April 3, H E W A S V E R Y S I C K.
   8 5 23 1 19 22 5 18 25 19 9 3 11

8. Harrison D I E D O F P N E U M O N I A.
   4 9 5 4 15 6 16 14 5 21 13 15 14 9 1

A - 1	N - 14
B - 2	O - 15
C - 3	P - 16
D - 4	Q - 17
E - 5	R - 18
F - 6	S - 19
G - 7	T - 20
H - 8	U - 21
I - 9	V - 22
J - 10	W - 23
K - 11	X - 24
L - 12	Y - 25
M - 13	Z - 26

John Tyler
1841–1845

CROSSWORD PUZZLE

ACROSS

4. Many people lost money when banks _____.
7. Tyler used courtesy and charm with people in U.S. and _____ countries.
8. John's father was a friend of Thomas _____.
11. 1816: Elected to U.S. House of _____.
14. Tyler was a governor's _____. (family member)
15. John and Father: both _____ (occupations)
16. Mother _____ when John was 7.
18. 1841: Tyler was _____ president.
19. Tyler: Famous as a skilled _____ (talker)
20. Some gov't officials wanted to im_____ him.
23. Learned to play the _____. (musical instrument)
25. 1827: Elected to the U.S. _____.
26. Tyler's parents: _____-to-do; owned much

DOWN

1. 1842: John's first _____ died.
2. Often used the _____ to reject bills.
3. Daughter Elizabeth: _____ at President's House. (wed)
5. Born at _____ Plantation.
6. _____ from Bank of the U.S. was put into some state banks.
9. Tyler averted _____ with England.
10. Home state: _____
12. John's parents were _____; showed the children much affection. (affectionate)
13. 1813: John married _____ Christian.
17. Birth_____: March 29, 1790
19. Had _____ brothers and sisters
21. 1825: John Quincy _____ was pres.
22. 1811: Elected to Virginia _____ of Delegates.
24. Tyler chose a _____ Cabinet after members resigned.

28

John Tyler
1841–1845

CROSSING OVER

DIRECTIONS
Use a pencil for this game. Using the words that are not in parentheses, find words from the following list that have the correct number of spaces and letters to fit into the crossing-over boxes. Each word has a place where it belongs. The first word is done for you. To continue, find a twelve-letter word having an "h" in the tenth space. All the words tell about John Tyler.

3 letters
few (people ever saw a president)
(studied) law
Kit (Carson: explorer)

4 letters
(father's name) John
(1832: Jackson tried to abolish) Bank (of the U.S.)
(1841: Tyler) vice (-pres.)

5 letters
(against) slave (auctions)
(preferred to do) right (than be popular)
panic (hit when banks failed)
(gov't money was put in) state (banks)
(China: open to U.S.) trade
(1844:) Texas (annexed to U.S.)
(plantations had a) dairy

(Tyler tried to) avert (war)
(each plantation had a pigeon) house

6 letters
(Julia:) second (wife)
(against) Africa (slave trade)
(money in state banks not handled) wisely
(Confederate forces fired on Ft.) Sumter

7 letters
Madison (was pres. while John was in Congress)
(1828) Jackson (president)
(Virginia) seceded (from Union)
(Tyler: called a) traitor (by Northern States)

8 letters
(elected) governor (of VA)
(his estate:) Sherwood (Forest)
(wanted) warships (built)
churches (started on frontier)
(birth state) Virginia
(Tyler ended) Seminole (war in FL)

9 letters
(plantations had) granaries
(Pres. Harrison died of) pneumonia
(1841: Tyler elected) president
(Tyler) predicted (the Civil War)
(plantations:) vegetable (gardens)

10 letters
depression (hit when banks failed)
steamboats (carried passengers and supplies)

12 letters
stagecoaches (traveled widely)

29

John Tyler
1841–1845

SAME FIRST LETTER
DIRECTIONS
Using words from any of the game pages about John Tyler, find two words that begin with the same letter for each of these letters. The circled letter is the first letter for each answer.

Example:

B R I T I S H
enemies of the colonies
E A R
forest animal

P _ _ _ _ _ _ _ _ _ _ _
a former capital of the colonies

_ _ _ _ _ _ _ _ _ _ _ _
a main avenue in Washington, D.C.

V _ _ _ _ _ _ _ _
Tyler's birth state

_ _ _ _ _ _ _
grown on Tyler's plantation

T _ _ _ _ _ _ _ _
Morse invented the _____ in 1837.

_ _ _ _ _ _ _
southern plantation crop

L _ _ _ _ _ _
was Tyler's first wife's name

_ _ _ _ _
Tyler's first occupation

C _ _ _ _ _ _ _ _ _ _
vehicles that traveled West

_ _ _ _ _
farm crop

F _ _ _ _ _ _ _ _
Oregon explorer

_ _ _ _ _ _ _
became a state in 1845

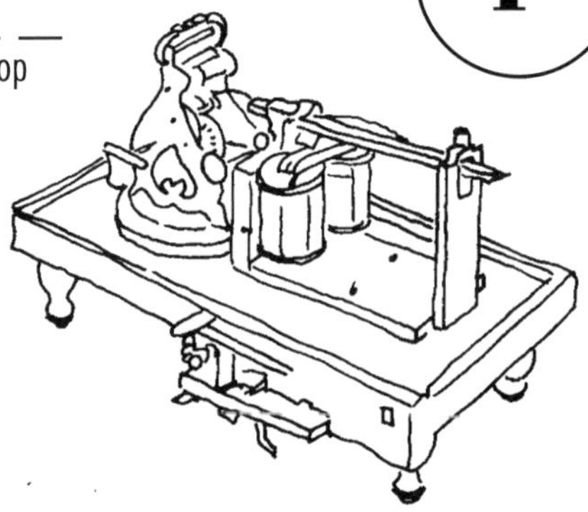

ALPHABET SEARCH
DIRECTIONS
Using words from any of the game pages about John Tyler, find words that begin with these letters of the alphabet.

A _____ H _____ O _____
B _____ I _____ P _____
C _____ J _____ R _____
D _____ K _____ S _____
E _____ L _____ T _____
F _____ M _____ V _____
G _____ N _____ W _____

James K. Polk
1845–1849

CROSSWORD PUZZLE

ACROSS

1. Retired from the presidency; became _____ (ill)
2. Liked these animals: _____
6. Birth state: North _____
8. The Polk family lived in a _____ cabin.
10. James met Sarah Childress again and fell in _____.
11. Mother's name: _____
12. At 17, James had an operation to remove gall _____.
14. Charlotte, NC, was about nine miles from the Polk _____. (barns, house, land)
16. As a lawyer, went on horse _____.
17. Polk was the _____ (number) president.
18. The Polk farm cabin faced Little _____ Creek.
19. At twenty-_____, he went to college.
20. Indian _____: no problem in their area (attacks)
22. 1819: Was clerk for Tennessee State _____.
24. Polk studied _____ books.
25. At voting places, a man's vote was given out _____. (by voice)
26. The Polks moved to land near _____, TN. (town)
28. Some Senators were rough _____ men. (settlers)

DOWN

1. At 17, James started _____, but learned quickly. (place of learning)
3. _____ man crossed the Polks' bridge once a week.
4. Lawyers and _____ (decided cases) stayed in county headquarters together.
5. Father's name: _____
7. James: born _____ 2, 1795
9. 1821: Was elected _____ of cavalry. (rank)
13. James was the _____ child in the family. (rank)
15. Polks' cabin had a _____ at each end.
18. James was born 1795, the year Tennessee became a _____.
21. As a boy, James was _____. (refers to size)
23. Backed people who would help the common _____.
25. James was well-_____.
27. Lawyers were needed to settle _____ titles.

31

James K. Polk
1845–1849

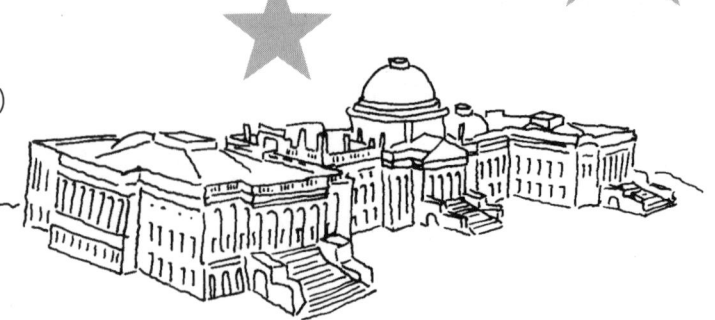

WORD SEARCHING
DIRECTIONS
In the grid, find these words about James K. Polk (the words that are not in parentheses). They can go up, down, across, at an angle, forward, or backward.

(1821: reelected) **clerk** (for Senate)

(had a) **good** (reputation)

(had a small law office; bought used) **law** (books)

(the Polks had) **no** (children)

(elected to TN) **legislature**

(was a tremendous) **speaker**

(Davy) **Crockett** (was a legislator with Polk)

(Polk helped Andrew) **Jackson** (become senator)

(James and Sarah) **married** (Jan. 1, 1824)

(Young Sarah had gone to an academy, for she was) **intelligent**

(1825: James elected to U.S.) **Congress**

(1825: U.S. Capitol was nearly) **rebuilt** (after British burned it in 1814)

(Congressmen stayed in boarding) **houses** (in Washington)

(Congress: in) **session** (Dec. through spring)

(Sarah went to Washington to hear James) **speak**

(summers and autumns; Sarah and James stayed in) **Tennessee**

(Polk: always interested in the) **common** (man)

(his speeches were short and to the) **point**

(1828: Jackson was elected) **president**

(Polk was the) **eleventh** (president)

(Henry Clay: Polk's) **enemy** (wanted high tariffs)

K	A	E	H	N	G	S	Q	Z	A	P	C	T
I	R	L	J	T	B	S	E	S	S	I	O	N
G	L	E	V	R	U	S	N	E	D	W	L	E
O	M	G	L	A	W	E	E	E	O	Y	X	G
O	N	I	B	C	F	R	M	S	I	K	D	I
D	C	S	K	G	P	G	Y	S	T	E	H	L
F	O	L	M	J	A	N	T	E	N	S	Q	L
B	J	A	C	K	S	O	N	N	E	U	C	E
I	E	T	L	R	O	C	S	N	D	G	N	T
H	N	U	K	M	T	D	R	E	I	S	T	N
T	H	R	T	P	T	Q	J	T	S	V	N	I
N	R	E	K	A	E	P	S	L	E	U	I	F
E	S	P	E	A	K	Y	U	I	R	C	O	T
V	A	Z	W	B	C	V	L	U	P	X	P	H
E	N	O	M	M	O	C	S	B	T	W	C	H
L	X	L	M	A	R	R	I	E	D	G	P	R
E	F	K	I	E	C	J	N	R	Y	M	D	Z

32

James K. Polk
1845–1849

NUMBER CODE
DIRECTIONS
Look at the numbers under each line. Find the matching numbers in the code box, and write the letters on the corresponding answer lines. All the sentences are about events during Polk's presidency.

1. There were bitter fights and debates on __ __ __ __ __ __ __.
   19 12 1 22 5 18 25

2. Sarah was an excellent __ __ __ __ __ __ __.
   8 15 19 20 5 19 19

3. Polk __ __ __ __ __ __ so hard he became __ __ __.
   23 15 18 11 5 4   9 12 12

4. The __ __ __ __ __ __ __ __ __ __ __ Institute was built.
   19 13 9 20 8 19 15 14 9 1 14

5. Sarah didn't allow dancing or __ __ __ __ playing at the President's House.
                                  3 1 18 4

6. The U.S. __ __ __ __ __ __ __ __ was built.
           20 18 5 1 19 21 18 25

7. The __ __ __ __ __ __ territory was annexed.
       15 18 5 7 15 14

8. Sarah was James's private __ __ __ __ __ __ __ __ __.
                              19 5 3 18 5 20 1 18 25

9. Areas that became states: __ __ __ __ __' __ __ __ __, Wisconsin
                              20 5 24 1 19   9 15 23 1

10. Polk refused to run for a __ __ __ __ __ __ __ term.
                               19 5 3 15 14 4

A - 1	N - 14
B - 2	O - 15
C - 3	P - 16
D - 4	Q - 17
E - 5	R - 18
F - 6	S - 19
G - 7	T - 20
H - 8	U - 21
I - 9	V - 22
J - 10	W - 23
K - 11	X - 24
L - 12	Y - 25
M - 13	Z - 26

SINGLE-LETTER WORDS
DIRECTIONS
Using any of the game pages about James K. Polk, find words about him that have letters of the alphabet used only once.
Example: oldest (Each letter is used one time only.)

_____ _____ _____ _____

_____ _____ _____ _____

_____ _____ _____ _____

_____ _____ _____ _____

_____ _____ _____ _____

33

Zachary Taylor
1849–1850

CROSSWORD PUZZLE

ACROSS

2. Kentucky farm near Ohio R. was a prosperous _____ plantation.
6. Capt. Taylor, with 50 men, held Ft. Harrison against 450 Indians and _____ Tecumseh.
7. Friends of Zach were _____ by Indians.
8. Zachary hunted raccoons and _____.
10. At 17: Swam across the Ohio _____ and back.
13. Born: _____ 24, 1784
16. Liked to _____ in the Ohio R.
17. He learned _____ and was patient. (quickly)
18. Pres. Madison was a second _____ of the Taylors. (relative)
20. Father's name: (Lt. Colonel) _____ Taylor
23. Richard built a log _____ in KY.
24. _____ howled at night near the cabin.
27. At 23, Zach joined the _____.
28. Zach and Margaret had _____ girls; one boy.
29. He was kind but could be _____ at times. (disagreeable)
30. Indians and the _____ fought Americans.
31. British soldiers marched from _____ to U.S.

DOWN

1. 1829: Two daughters _____ of fever.
3. Margaret and _____: with Zach at his stations
4. Became _____ for bravery and ability. (well-known)
5. Wife's name: _____
9. Zach: Born while parents traveled toward _____. (state)
11. Birth state: _____
12. British and Indians captured U.S. _____. (military constructions)
14. Richard: Given 6,000 acres of _____ for service in Revolutionary War.
15. The infantry: He began as a _____. (rank)
19. Daughter, _____, married Lt. Jefferson Davis.
21. Often, _____ hid nearby in Kentucky.
22. As a child, Zach played _____ with his friends. (army term)
25. 1811: Capt. Taylor was sent to Ft. Knox in _____. (state)
26. Kentucky: His parents put _____ on doors and windows at night for protection.

Zachary Taylor
1849–1850

SUPPLY THE VOWEL
DIRECTIONS
In the grid, look for the following words (the words that are not in parentheses). The words can go up, down, across, at angles, backward, or forward. Parts of words may overlap. Supply the correct vowel—a e i o u—for the center of each word group.

(Brig. General Taylor was called "Old) **Rough** (and Ready)"

(Taylor) **bought** (a second Mississippi plantation)

(Zachary saw son-)**in**(-law, Jefferson Davis, in war in Mexico)

(Taylor purchased a) **cotton** (plantation in Louisiana)

(Taylor and troops had two weeks to) **repair** (Ft. Knox)

(Sarah, wife of Jefferson Davis) **died** (in Mississippi)

(Taylor's Mississippi plantation had live)**stock**

R	A	G	S	W	C	Q	I	L	U	E	T	Y
M	E	L	A	K	A	F	B	C	I	G	J	F
H	S	P	R	H	P	V	R	H	K	N	G	S
D	T	R	○	P	P	E	R	S	A	X	○	T
O	J	W	H	I	L	Q	B	W	D	C	N	N
N	K	D	S	U	R	S	N	Y	R	V	G	F
R	B	E	O	D	T	C	G	O	T	E	L	P
N	O	T	T	○	C	L	F	R	I	J	A	A
H	M	U	C	S	W	B	S	L	P	R	N	F
V	O	K	W	C	K	A	O	O	O	B	D	C
N	S	L	T	E	Y	K	C	○	T	N	E	K
D	E	○	D	O	M	E	G	I	G	K	O	G
F	N	N	V	L	D	H	I	S	E	H	U	W
H	L	C	N	A	T	Q	D	I	J	R	T	M
S	A	O	M	B	D	Y	K	A	L	C	A	O
Z	G	L	F	Q	R	P	O	N	S	T	V	C
P	I	N	H	Y	J	E	W	A	B	D	U	N

(Jefferson) **Davis** (later became Confederate pres.)

(Mexicans ambushed) **forces** (under Capt. Thornton)

(1812: United States at war with) **England**

(Abraham) **Lincoln** (was congressman when Taylor was nominated for pres.)

(Zach's Mississippi plantation sold) **wood** (to steamboats)

Sarah (the Taylors' daughter)

(1819: Lt. Col. Taylor was sent to) **Louisiana**

(Seminole Indian chief) **Osceola**

(Gen. Taylor wore baggy old cotton and) **linen** (clothes)

(Major Taylor was sent to protect) **trappers** (in Wisconsin)

(1824: Zach transferred to) **Kentucky**

(1832: Black) **Hawk** (wanted land back and killed settlers)

(1845: Taylor protected) **Texas** (at southern border)

35

Zachary Taylor
1849–1850

SKYSCRAPER

DIRECTIONS

Write your answers in the boxes. The circled letters will help you.

1. Mrs. Taylor was not _____ when she moved into the President's House. (health)
2. She stayed in a bedroom, because she didn't _____ Washington.
3. Pres. Taylor's daughter, _____, was hostess for dinners at the President's House.
4. 1849: United States was very prosperous, with _____ growing in the South and textile mills in the North. (an export)
5. Extreme anger over slavery caused fistfights and gun-carrying in the _____ in the Capitol building.
6. Pres. Taylor did not want the _____ split.
7. Pres. Taylor developed signs of cholera and _____ fever.
8. The president died and his vice-president, Millard _____, became president.
9. Pres. Taylor's horse, Old _____, walked behind the coffin.
10. Later, Taylor was reburied at his plantation in _____. (state)

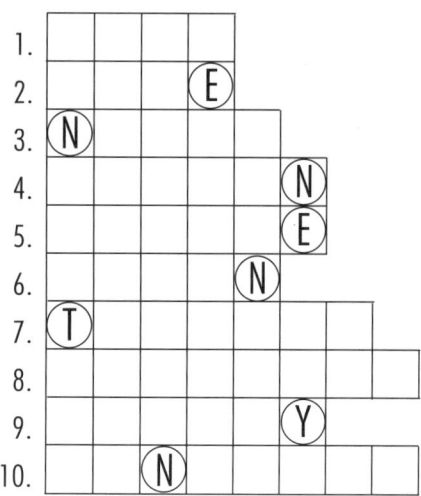

NUMBER CODE

DIRECTIONS

Look at the numbers under each line. Find the matching numbers in the code box, and write the letters on the corresponding answer lines.

Something happened during Zachary Taylor's term as president. What was it?

__ __ 1850, __ __ __ __ __ __ __ __ __ __ __ __ __ __ __
9 14   20 8 5 6 9 18 19 20 15 22 5 18 12 1 14 4

__ __ __ __ __ __ __ __ __ __ __ __ __ __ __ . __ __
13 1 9 12   19 5 18 22 9 3   5 2 5 7 1 14   9 20

__ __ __ __ __ __ __ __ __ __ __ __ __ __ __ __ __ __ __ to __ __ __
23 5 14 20   6 18 15 13   13 9 19 19 15 21 18 9   14 5 23

__ __ __ __ __ __ . It took about thirty days.
13 5 24 9 3 15

A - 1	N - 14
B - 2	O - 15
C - 3	P - 16
D - 4	Q - 17
E - 5	R - 18
F - 6	S - 19
G - 7	T - 20
H - 8	U - 21
I - 9	V - 22
J - 10	W - 23
K - 11	X - 24
L - 12	Y - 25
M - 13	Z - 26

Millard Fillmore
1850–1853

CROSSWORD PUZZLE

ACROSS
5. 1823: Millard was a well-known _____. (profession)
6. 1841: Vice-Pres. _____ was inaugurated president.
8. As a boy, he sometimes went _____ and fishing.
10. Had _____ brothers and sisters.
11. 1828: A _____, Millard Powers Fillmore, was born.
12. Millard moved to Buffalo, _____ school, and studied law.
14. Born: _____ 7, 1800
17. Mother's name: _____
19. 1842: He was praised for good handling of gov't; Great Depression began to _____.
20. Millard's parents were _____ farmers. (no money)
23. Born 1832: a _____, Mary Abigail (Abby)
24. Pres. Jackson took gov't. _____ from the Bank of the U.S.
26. Millard was reelected to _____.
27. He worked with the N.Y. _____ Supreme Court.
28. 1841: William H. _____ was inaugurated pres.

DOWN
1. Fillmore: known for his _____ character. (outstanding)
2. 1826: Millard and Abigail, his former teacher, were _____.
3. At 15, he was _____ and able to do farm work well. (powerful)
4. As a law apprentice; he worked for a greedy, rich _____ with no compassion for the poor. (made law decisions)
7. Fillmore believed in states' _____. (authority)
9. Father's name: _____
11. At 19, Millard attended _____; his teacher was 21.
13. Father moved his family nearer Buffalo, New _____.
15. 1833: Fillmore was sent as a _____ to Washington.
16. Sen. Webster helped connect Millard to the _____ Court. (highest)
18. As a boy, Millard worked _____. (diligently)
21. Fillmore worked hard for the _____. (party)
22. Bought law _____ and studied intensely.
25. 1841: Chairman of the Ways and _____ Committee
26. Millard Fillmore was born in a log _____.

37

Millard Fillmore
1850–1853

CROSSING OVER

DIRECTIONS
Use a pencil for this game. Using the words that are not in parentheses, find words from the following list that have the correct number of spaces and letters to fit into the crossing-over boxes. Each word has a place where it belongs. The first word is done for you. To continue, find an eleven-letter word having an "r" in the eleventh space. All the words tell about Millard Fillmore.

3 letters
- (as a boy, mowed) hay
- (Millard's wisdom brought Depression to an) end
- (Buffalo, NY:) law (practice flourished)
- (wife, Abigail, was) ill

4 letters
- (1800: Fillmore) born
- (as a boy, used a wooden) plow
- (as a boy, pulled plow by) mule
- (as a boy, hauled wood) home
- (Thurlow) Weed (an underhanded character)
- (1849: Taylor was pres., Fillmore) vice (-pres.)

5 letters
- (as a boy, reaped) wheat
- (as a boy, cut down) trees
- (daughter Abby liked) music (lessons)
- (slavery) hotly (argued in western areas)
- (truly desired) peace (for the Union)
- (passed wise) bills (on slavery)

6 letters
- (as a boy, pulled tree) stumps
- (elected State Assemblyman for) Albany (NY)
- (spent much time with his) family
- (1800: largest U.S. export) cotton

7 letters
- (very attentive to wife) Abigail
- (big issue in politics:) slavery
- (Daniel) Webster (secretary of state)
- (Abby, 19, helped with) hostess (duties at President's House)
- (Weed tried, underhandedly, to) destroy (Fillmore)

8 letters
- (1842:) Millard didn't run for) Congress
- (he) disliked (slavery)
- (people were) grateful (to Fillmore for saving the Union)

9 letters
- (Millard's son was his private) secretary
- (1800, Fillmore's birth year, Johnny) Appleseed (roamed Ohio Valley)

10 letters
- (U.S.) prosperity (increased)
- (learned new words from a) dictionary
- (1800: U.S. capital moved from Philadelphia to) Washington

11 letters
- (Millard's great-) grandfather (escaped from pirates)

38

Millard Fillmore
1850–1853

NAME THE BILL

DIRECTIONS

Fill in the dotted lines with your answers. If they are correct, the circled letters will spell the name of the bill that was presented before Congress and was aimed at pleasing both North and South.

1. Fillmore _____ American business trade overseas. (urged)
2. In appreciation for Fillmore's wisdom in office, some New York merchants gave Abigail a magnificent coach and two fine _____.
3. Fillmore didn't want a second _____ as president.
4. Fillmore wanted Peary to go to Japan; later, two _____ were opened to U.S. trade.
5. _____ was still a bitter issue.
6. Fillmore believed that seizing land belonging to other _____ was dishonorable. (nations)
7. Thurlow Weed's followers tried to defeat Millard _____'s reelection. (last name)
8. _____ was defeated for reelection. (first name)
9. When Abigail and daughter Abby died, Millard was very _____. (broken-hearted)
10. Hawaii was willing to be _____ to the U.S.
11. 1858: Fillmore married _____ MacIntosh, a widow.
12. Fillmore and his second wife lived in _____, NY.

1. _ _ ◯ _ _ _ _ _ _
2. _ ◯ _ _ _ _
3. _ _ ◯ _
4. ◯ _ _ _ _
5. _ _ _ _ ◯ _
6. _ ◯ _ _ _ _ _ _ _
7. _ _ _ _ ◯ _ _ _ ' _
8. _ _ _ ◯ _ _ _
9. _ _ _ ◯ _ _
10. _ _ _ _ ◯
11. _ _ ◯ _ _
12. _ _ ◯ _ _ _

1850

CLUE

DIRECTIONS

Each set of lines has a vowel and an occasional consonant to help you determine the correct answer. All the words tell about Millard and Abigail Fillmore.

1. Abigail had the first   b a __ __ __ u __   put into the President's House.
2. Abigail caught a cold at Pierce's   i __ __ u __ u __ __ __ __ o __   and died.
3. The   __ i __ i __   War began in 1861.
4. Fillmore said he only took one dose of   __ e __ i __ i __ e   in thirty years.
5. 1874: Fillmore had a   s t __ o __ e.
6. March 1874: Fillmore had a   __ e c __ __ d   stroke and died.

39

Franklin Pierce
1853–1857

CROSSWORD PUZZLE

ACROSS

2. 1824: Franklin was _____ in Hillsborough, NH. (top U.S. postal job)
5. Was born in a log _____.
7. His _____, Benjamin, was 18 in 1775. (close family member)
9. Travelers stopping at father's home brought the latest _____.
11. Wife Jane's second son, 4, _____.
12. Franklin's oldest _____ fought in War of 1812.
14. Had _____ brothers and sisters.
18. Birth state: New _____.
19. Father in battle of Valley _____.
22. 1821: Work began on the _____ Rd., linking Maryland to Illinois.
24. 1775: Paul _____ warned Benjamin the British were coming.
25. The Pierces' first _____ died after three days.
27. After Franklin's birth, the family moved to _____, NH.
28. 1833: Franklin was elected to _____ in Washington.
29. Congressmen _____ over the slavery issue. (clashed)

DOWN

1. His father's home was also a _____. (business)
3. Benjamin Pierce, like Jefferson, believed in _____' rights.
4. 1821: 360 miles of _____ Canal were nearly finished.
6. 1827: Father was _____ of NH. (top job)
8. Father told many _____ War stories.
10. Travelers stopping at the Pierces' home often _____ overnight.
13. Mother's name: _____.
15. As a boy he shot a gun, hunted, _____, and trapped animals for food.
16. Commodore Perry, with a U.S. _____, visited Japan. (ships)
17. George Washington called Benjamin an excellent _____.
20. 1814: Lawyer _____ Scott Key wrote the "Star-Spangled Banner" on an old envelope.
21. 1825: Franklin moved to _____, NH.
23. Father was a farmer, councilman, sheriff, Brig. Gen'l of State _____. (forces)
26. 1824: When Franklin graduated from college, James _____ was president.

40

Franklin Pierce
1853–1857

WORD SEARCHING
DIRECTIONS
In the grid, find these words about Franklin Pierce (the words that are not in parentheses). They can go up, down, across, at an angle, forward, or backward.

A	R	E	C	L	A	T	T	O	R	N	E	Y
B	E	N	J	A	M	I	N	P	O	B	G	D
F	B	R	I	W	H	K	R	S	T	M	R	J
Q	M	Y	U	A	N	Z	K	J	A	N	E	L
V	E	S	B	T	D	C	X	O	E	C	K	U
G	V	F	W	I	A	M	O	H	P	K	A	J
Q	O	N	S	J	U	L	Y	V	A	T	E	R
A	N	U	E	W	J	B	S	R	H	G	P	I
D	F	C	T	L	K	M	E	I	E	L	S	G
E	N	P	Q	D	S	L	U	L	G	O	V	T
T	W	Y	A	C	O	D	L	B	R	E	G	S
C	J	O	K	H	P	O	F	I	L	N	L	H
E	D	Q	C	R	C	B	R	E	T	A	U	M
L	M	E	X	I	C	O	A	S	V	E	C	V
E	S	A	R	O	T	A	N	E	S	H	I	G
E	F	Y	D	W	K	D	R	O	C	N	O	C
R	J	O	M	N	Q	Y	T	P	S	O	L	R

(Franklin born) **November** (23, 1804)

(father's name:) **Benjamin**

(Franklin spent much time) **outdoors** (as a child)

(1809: Franklin in N.H.) **legislature**

(1820: he went to Bowdoin) **College** (in Maine)

(1824: he began studying) **law**

(1829:) **Jackson** (was president; Benjamin was governor)

(1831: Pierce elected) **Speaker** (of the House in NH)

(1832: Pierce) **reelected** (Speaker of the House in NH)

(1833: Pierce ill with) **cholera**

(1834: Franklin married) **Jane** (Appleton)

(1836: Congress fighting over) **slavery**

(1837: Franklin was elected) **Senator**

(1842: Pierce resigned from Senate, went to) **Concord** (as a lawyer)

(Pres. Polk made Pierce Federal) **Attorney** (for NH)

(1846: war with) **Mexico**

Presidential Puzzlers Copyright © 2005 Good Year Books

41

Franklin Pierce
1853–1857

SAME FIRST LETTER
DIRECTIONS
Using words from any of the game pages about Pierce, find two words that begin with the same letter for each of these letters. The circled letter is the first letter for each answer.

Example:

P
P E R R Y — Naval commodore
P I E R C E — not reelected president

S _ _ _ _ _ - _ _ _ _ age of Pierce at death
_ _ _ _ _ Wrote *Uncle Tom's Cabin*.

C _ _ _ _ _ _ _ _ Pierce was born in it.
_ _ _ _ _ _ _ _ Pierce retired there.

T _ _ _ _ _ Pierce's son killed on it.
_ _ _ _ _ _ Agreed to, by Japan and U.S.

U _ _ _ _ _ _ _ _ _ _ men with evil intent
_ _ _ _ _ _ _ _ _ _ _ (human) railroad

B _ _ _ _ _ Killed five proslavers.
_ _ _ _ _ _ _ feelings about slavery

K _ _ _ _ _ _ state divided by slavery
_ _ _ _ _ _ This happened to 200 Kansas men.

NUMBER CODE
DIRECTIONS
Look at the numbers under each line. Find the matching numbers in the code box, and write the letters on the corresponding answer lines.

1. 1856: Proslavery Congressman Brooks, with his C A N E   N E A R L Y   K I L L E D
   3 1 14 5   14 5 1 18 12 25   11 9 12 12 5 4

   antislavery Senator Sumner, and it took T H R E E   Y E A R S for Sumner to recover.
   20 8 18 5 5   25 5 1 18 19

2. 1856: B U C H A N A N was elected president, N O T
   2 21 3 8 1 14 1 14   14 15 20

   P I E R C E
   16 9 5 18 3 5

3. 1853: Jane Pierce was V E R Y   I L L after her third and only remaining son, Benjamin,
   22 5 18 25   9 12 12

   D I E D in a T R A I N A C C I D E N T.
   4 9 5 4   20 18 1 9 14 1 3 3 9 4 5 14 20

4. After one term in office, Franklin and Jane went to E U R O P E   F O R
   5 21 18 15 16 5   6 15 18

   T H R E E   Y E A R S. He D I E D I N 1869.
   20 8 18 5 5   25 5 1 18 19   4 9 5 4 9 14

A – 1	N – 14
B – 2	O – 15
C – 3	P – 16
D – 4	Q – 17
E – 5	R – 18
F – 6	S – 19
G – 7	T – 20
H – 8	U – 21
I – 9	V – 22
J – 10	W – 23
K – 11	X – 24
L – 12	Y – 25
M – 13	Z – 26

James Buchanan
1857–1861

CROSSWORD PUZZLE

ACROSS

5. 1819: James met Ann and fell in _____.
7. 1845: Was secretary of state for Pres. _____
8. Ancestors came from _____. (country)
11. In 1821, most Americans _____. (occupation)
12. Federalists believed in strong central gov't with fewer _____ rights.
13. James learned to save and use money _____.
14. White men, rich or poor, allowed to _____.
16. Buchanan, minister to Russia, was well-liked by _____ Nicholas.
20. 1830: The _____ population was harshly pushed west.
21. Father, in his store, learned to keep _____ accounts. (precise)
23. 1821: James was elected to _____.
25. James was a _____, like George Washington. (party member)
26. Later years: an _____ statesman (older)
27. He was the _____ for a judge and won the case. (pleader)

DOWN

1. Many _____ came to the U.S. from other countries.
2. (1821) New _____: largest U.S. city
3. 1821: Buchanan was taking _____ of his brothers and sisters.
4. 1815: Was nominated State _____ for Lancaster County, PA.
6. Mother's name: _____
7. Birth state: _____
9. Some Americans wanted to send freed _____ to Liberia, Africa.
10. Men gathered in father's store to discuss _____ and politics.
15. While pres.: he gave a _____ 3¢ when the man undercharged him.
17. _____, Buchanan's fiancée, died.
18. During walks in woods, he practiced _____ about law. (talking)
19. He learned law in _____, PA. (capital)
22. James was _____ and tall, earned a good living, and was attractive to young ladies. (good-looking)
23. 1809: Lancaster, PA: biggest U.S. _____ located inland.
24. 1812: James was a _____. (occupation)
25. A wise, thorough lawyer; won _____. (distinction)

James Buchanan
1857–1861

SUPPLY THE VOWEL
DIRECTIONS
In the grid, look for the following words (the words that are not in parentheses). The words can go up, down, across, at angles, backward, or forward. Parts of words may overlap. Supply the correct vowel—a e i o u—for the center of each word group.

- (1821) **fur** (traders in the Northwest)
- (James appointed minister to) **Russia**
- (1848: he bought) **Wheatland** (an estate)
- (took homeless nieces and nephews into his) **home**
- (he joined the) **militia** (when the British threatened Baltimore)
- (great) **anger** (over slaves and free states)
- (James's housekeeper: Miss) **Hetty**
- (Harriet, James's niece, was popular as hostess and First) **Lady** (for her uncle)
- (he liked sauerkraut and) **potatoes**
- (James, secretary of state, was tired and) **sick**
- (niece, Harriet was a great) **success** (in England)
- (Buchanan never) **married**
- **Harriet** (arranged a reception for a Japanese delegation)
- (both James's housekeeper and his) **niece** (attended the Inaugural Ball)
- (was the first time photographs were taken of an Inaugural) **Ball**
- (James) **bought** (Ann Coleman's former home)
- (a steamship was named U.S.S. *Harriet Lane* in his niece's) **honor**
- (1852: Pierce was pres.; Buchanan was) **minister** (to England)
- (1858: great anger over) **slavery**
- (Harriet) **worked** (for better conditions for the Indians)

A	D	H	L	E	B	Y	A	W	U	S	K	C
H	L	L	J	G	L	R	R	H	H	A	D	V
M	○	R	R	I	E	D	R	○	G	N	A	T
B	D	R	P	F	T	O	T	A	V	K	C	Y
M	Y	B	R	H	G	T	N	T	L	A	O	M
E	R	S	G	I	Y	J	F	L	W	A	L	C
I	F	○	R	S	E	P	N	A	Q	I	A	S
H	O	C	S	U	B	T	W	N	Y	T	F	R
B	V	C	O	S	L	D	E	D	M	I	C	O
H	D	E	J	P	I	R	W	T	S	L	M	U
K	E	S	Y	D	C	A	E	C	E	○	N	O
A	K	S	E	H	T	G	J	L	N	M	C	M
H	R	M	P	V	K	R	U	I	Y	I	V	K
P	○	T	A	T	O	E	S	R	B	N	S	Z
H	W	N	D	B	I	T	F	A	T	F	U	N
G	E	H	O	M	E	V	J	C	L	O	B	P
A	S	K	N	R	T	S	W	I	E	W	D	Y

44

James Buchanan
1857–1861

SCRAMBLED WORDS
DIRECTIONS
Unscramble the words and write the answers on the lines provided. (Use scrap paper to work out your answers.)

1. The spoils EMSTSY rewarded supporters with government jobs. _____
2. A Boston minister, William Garrison, printed an antislavery RAPEP every week and was attacked. _____
3. An antislavery Quaker teacher, Prudence Crandall, allowed black girls in her school and was sent to ISRNOP. _____
4. At Wheatland, Buchanan's estate, many political friends asked his CIAEVD. _____
5. For the first time ever, photographs were EATNK at the Inaugural Ball. _____
6. April 1861: Confederate forces attacked Ft. MTSREU. _____

HOME AND SCHOOL PAIRS
DIRECTIONS
All the Buchanan home and school words in the large box are written twice, except for one. Write the name of each pair on a line. (Cross off the pairs as you find them.) Then find the name of the home and school word that appears only once, and write it in the box.

Abraham Lincoln
1861–1865

CROSSWORD PUZZLE

ACROSS

6. 1816: State of Indiana did not _____ slavery. (permit)
8. Later, he had a _____ mother.
10. _____: Made from blackberry juice; pens from feathers.
11. Read a biography of George _____.
13. As a boy carried _____ from the fireplace.
15. 1812: Travelers to Lexington, KY, passed the Lincolns' _____. (house, barn, land)
17. Abe cut many trees with an _____; worked hard.
18. 1786: An _____ shot Lincoln's grandfather.
20. To Abe _____ was evil.
22. Abe had an older sister, _____.
25. Thomas was a friend of Daniel _____. (frontiersman)
26. Birthplace: Hodgenville, _____.
27. Abe loved to _____ books.
28. Learned to _____ his kind stepmother.

DOWN

1. 1816: Father claimed _____ in Indiana.
2. Abe and Sarah learned the _____ and numbers in school.
3. Abe axed trees and became very _____.
4. He _____ wood for fences.
5. 1818: Abe's mother, Nancy, died of _____ sickness.
7. He ground corn for _____.
9. Young Abe gathered _____ and berries.
12. Studied _____ and watched lawyers at work.
14. At 19: Went down the Ohio R. to New Orleans on a _____.
15. Born: _____ 12, 1809
16. Winter: Abe and Sarah walked four _____ to a log school.
19. 1830: Thomas moved family to Illinois with oxen and _____.
21. Father, Thomas, moved family to KY; built a _____.
23. Abe: Seriously ill after a _____ kicked his head.
24. Thomas hunted deer and _____.

Presidential Puzzlers Copyright © 2005 Good Year Books

Abraham Lincoln
1861–1865

CROSSING OVER

DIRECTIONS
Use a pencil for this game. Using the words that are not in parentheses, find words from the following list that have the correct number of spaces and letters to fit into the crossing-over boxes. Each word has a place where it belongs. The first word is done for you. To continue, find a ten-letter word having an "n" in the tenth space. All the words tell about Abraham Lincoln.

3 letters
(When Mother died, Sarah, 12, took care of) **Abe** (and father)
(Col. Robert E.) **Lee** (captured John Brown)

4 letters
(Abe planted) **corn**
(1839: Abe met) **Mary** (Todd)
(1843: Lincoln's son, Robert, was) **born**
(Abe was very) **kind**
(Abe and Mary had four) **sons**
(1850: the Lincolns' son, Eddie, 4,) **died**

5 letters
(1807: Abe's sister) **Sarah** (born)
(Abe helped) **plant** (beans)
(Abe read the) **Bible**
(Abe did not) **drink** (liquor)
(Abe joked; made people) **laugh**
(Abe felt very) **plain**

6 letters
(Abe: always) **honest**
(1837: Abe became a) **lawyer**
(Slavery: a) **bitter** (battle)
(1857: Lincoln in U.S.) **Senate**
(Abe wanted black people to have basic) **rights**
(Kentucky cabin where Abe was born is now in a) **museum**

7 letters
(Abe was hard)**working**
(1842: Abe) **married** (Mary)
(Lincoln: made strong speeches against) **slavery**

8 letters
(Abe planted) **potatoes**
(1846: Abe elected to) **Congress**

9 letters
(Lincoln-Douglas debates got national) **attention**
(1860: Lincoln elected) **president**

10 letters
(Lincoln was made) **postmaster** (in New Salem, IL)
(1847: Lincolns moved to) **Washington**
(Sally, Abe's) **stepmother** (was very kind)

11 letters
(Lincoln: elected four times to state) **legislature**
(law practice:) **Springfield** (capital of IL)

47

Abraham Lincoln
1861–1865

HOW LINCOLN FELT ABOUT THE SOUTH

DIRECTIONS

Fill in the dotted lines with your answers. If they are correct, the circled letters will tell how Lincoln felt about the South after the Civil War.

1. Bitter conflict over slavery led to the Civil _____.
2. Abe bought his first home in _____, IL.
3. The Lincolns' first son's name: _____
4. When Abe and Mary moved into their house, their baby son was nine _____ old.
5. Only their oldest son lived to become a _____.
6. Their second son, _____, was four when he died.
7. Third son, _____, died in the President's House.
8. Fourth son, Tad, became _____ and died at 18.
9. Lincoln was a very _____ lawyer.
10. Abe was an _____ lawyer; people trusted him.
11. 1847: Lincoln was _____ to Congress.
12. The Mexican War was _____ by the U.S. Armies. (victorious)
13. To Lincoln slavery was _____.
14. Abe debated slavery with Stephen _____.
15. Before his inauguration, South _____ seceded from the Union.
16. 1860: Lincoln was elected _____.
17. At Springfield, Lincoln said, "I bid you an affectionate farewell," and he left for _____.
18. Enroute to Washington, Abe learned of a _____ to kill him.
19. 1861: Lincoln was _____ president.
20. He was the _____ (number) president.

48

Andrew Johnson
1865–1869

CROSSWORD PUZZLE

ACROSS

3. _____, newspapers, speeches read to tailors as they worked. (printed volumes)
5. Father's name: _____
6. Jacob rescued two drowning _____; later, he died.
11. Andy met _____ and fell in love.
13. Birth state: North _____
15. Andy took his _____ mother to Greeneville, TN. (weary)
16. 1832: Daughter, _____, was born.
17. Jacob and his family: _____ (little money)
19. Andy was very _____. (character trait)
21. Pres. Jackson had been poor; he was Andy's _____. (model)
22. Eliza taught Andy to _____. (with pen)
24. Andy tailored clothes by _____. (no machines)
27. 1828: Daughter, _____, was born.
28. 1834: Son, _____, was born.
29. In Greeneville, TN, Andy got a tailoring _____.
31. 1835: Was elected to _____ Legislature.
32. Andy's parents were called _____, due to earth floors, doorways.

DOWN

1. 1808: Son Andrew was _____.
2. At 18, Andy _____ Eliza, 16. (wed)
4. Andy: too poor to attend _____.
7. He became a skilled _____. (sewing cloth)
8. He taught himself to _____.
9. Mother, Mary, took in _____ for wealthy people. (laundry)
10. Jacob was a _____ at an inn. (served)
12. Eliza, intelligent, managed their money _____. (with wisdom)
14. Mary wove _____ to sell.
18. William: Andy's older _____.
20. 1828: Andy was _____ to town council.
21. People in Greeneville worked _____. (diligently)
23. 1830: Son, _____, was born.
25. Had a great _____ to learn. (yearning)
26. Andy gave great _____.
27. 1830: Andy elected as Greeneville's _____. (town leader)
30. Andy bought his mother a small _____. (with barn and house)

Andrew Johnson
1865–1869

WORD SEARCHING
DIRECTIONS
In the grid, find these words about Andrew Johnson (the words that are not in parentheses). They can go up, down, across, at an angle, forward, or backward.

- (1831: Andy bought the first real) **house** (he ever lived in)
- (1841: Andy elected to) **Tennessee** (Senate)
- (slavery was a bitter) **issue**
- (Andy worked to help the laboring) **people**
- (1843: Andy elected to U.S.) **Congress**
- (Andy loved the) **Library** (of Congress and read much)
- (Andy: elected to Congress again; brought daughter,) **Martha,** (18, with him)
- (1851: Andy bought a large) **brick** (house for his family)
- (the Johnsons' last child) **Andrew** (born)
- (1853: Andy was elected) **governor** (of TN)
- (Andy: a powerful) **speaker**
- (he worked hard to earn a good) **living**
- (the) **common** (people liked Andy)
- (Jacob, Andy's father, was of English, Scottish, and) **Irish** (descent)
- (William, Andy's brother, was a) **printing** (apprentice, also)
- (William and Andy had tailoring) **apprenticeships**
- (Andy opened a tailoring shop in) **Carthage,** (NC)
- (did not try to help the) **wealthy**

C	P	B	E	H	K	T	A	G	U	Q	I	D
N	R	L	P	R	O	J	P	E	O	P	L	E
F	I	R	I	S	H	W	A	S	D	M	V	S
B	N	F	R	J	L	E	N	U	Y	O	C	P
K	T	G	O	S	M	I	L	O	W	B	Y	I
P	I	Q	N	T	R	H	B	H	M	N	S	H
A	N	D	R	E	W	A	Z	R	C	M	V	S
X	G	U	E	D	T	H	P	I	A	A	O	E
F	I	E	V	L	E	G	A	H	T	R	A	C
M	J	U	O	K	N	O	R	G	N	T	Y	I
E	U	S	G	I	N	T	Z	Y	D	H	A	T
B	Y	S	V	W	E	C	B	H	E	A	G	N
R	V	I	H	J	S	L	N	T	S	K	M	E
I	L	R	T	Q	S	Y	O	L	W	A	F	R
C	O	N	G	R	E	S	S	A	D	B	S	P
K	P	I	S	P	E	A	K	E	R	G	I	P
U	L	H	C	K	V	F	M	W	J	N	E	A

Andrew Johnson
1865–1869

WAR YEARS SKYSCRAPER
DIRECTIONS
Write your answers in the boxes. The circled letters will help you.

1. 1861: _____ (number) states seceded from the Union.
2. Jefferson Davis _____ was the Confederate president.
3. The South _____ on Ft. Sumter.
4. Johnson's son, Charles, was a doctor for the _____ army.
5. 1862: Lincoln named Johnson the Military _____ of Tennessee. (head)
6. The Johnsons' son _____ died.
7. 1863: Lincoln declared the _____ in rebel states free.
8. 1865: Lincoln was reelected; _____ became vice-president.
9. 1865: Lincoln was shot; Johnson became _____.

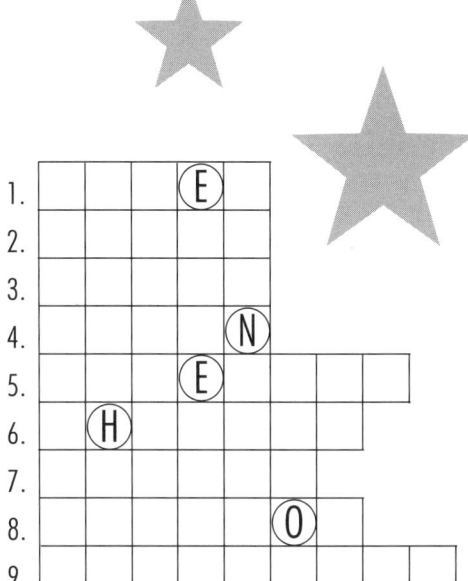

CLUE
DIRECTIONS
Each set of lines has vowels and an occasional consonant to help you determine the correct answer. All the words tell about Andrew Johnson.

1. 1865: Eliza was ill with   __ u __ e __ __ u __ o __ i __.
2. 1865: Martha, the Johnsons' daughter, was   __ o s __ e __ __   at the President's House.
3. Martha, at the President's House, often   m e __ __ e __   her own dresses and   __ i __ __ e __   the two cows kept on the grounds of the President's House.
4. Johnson followed Lincoln's desire to treat the   __ o u __ __   with   __ i n __ __ e __ __.
5. Some Washington men made fun of Andy's poor   b a __ __ __ __ o u __ __.
6. 1866: White men in the   __ u __ __ u __ __ a __   dressed as ghosts to frighten free black men and treated them cruelly.
7. 1867: Congress refused to follow Lincoln's and Johnson's plans for   r e __ o __ __ __ __ u __ __ i o __.
8. Radicals, members of a political party who were enemies of Johnson, tried to   i __ __ e a __ __   him, but failed.
9. 1868: U __ y __ __ e __ __. __ __ a __ __   was elected U.S. president.
10. 1875: Johnson was again elected to the   U. __. __ e __ a __ e.
11. 1875: Johnson died. His body was wrapped in a   U. __. __ __ a __   and buried in   G __ e e __ e __ i __ __ e, __ e __ __ e __ __ e e.

Ulysses S. Grant
1869–1877

CROSSWORD PUZZLE

ACROSS

1. West Point: Grant treated everyone _____. (impartially)
4. Grant's father, Jesse, owned a _____, where he treated leather.
5. Ulysses liked to ride a _____, fish, and swim.
9. At 7, he plowed _____.
10. Jesse: known for _____ in business (character trait)
13. Ulysses born: _____ 27, 1822
14. He met Julia _____ in St. Louis.
15. Went to West _____ Military Academy in NY.
18. As a child, he attended _____ in a frontier settlement.
19. The _____ and South conflict grew worse.
23. He trained the St. Louis militia and did a great _____.
24. 1848: Ulysses and Julia were _____.
25. At West Point, Grant liked _____. (school subject)
28. At 7, he worked _____ wood in his wagon. (carrying)
29. He captured Ft. _____ and Ft. Henry.

DOWN

1. He always tried to _____ what he started.
2. West Point: Learned about waging _____. (battles)
3. West Point: Grant _____ others' rights. (honored)
6. He always _____ his parents. (did what they asked)
7. At 10 he was _____ by travelers for transportation to distant places. (paid)
8. Father's name: _____
11. Birth state: _____
12. Mother's name: _____
16. At 12: an accomplished _____ (rider)
17. After _____, he was sent from West Point to St. Louis, MO. (finishing school)
20. At West Point, he was _____. (character trait)
21. Julia's brother, _____, was Grant's friend.
22. Mother, Hannah, was very _____.
24. Lt. Grant fought bravely in the _____ War.
26. Grant was _____-working. (diligent)
27. He had _____ younger brothers and sisters.

52

Ulysses S. Grant
1869–1877

SUPPLY THE VOWEL
DIRECTIONS
In the grid, look for the following words (the words that are not in parentheses). The words can go up, down, across, at angles, backward, or forward. Parts of words may overlap. Supply the correct vowel——a e i o u——for the center of each word group.

S	A	E	G	B	C	M	J	H	D	E	R	S
L	W	P	G	D	E	T	C	E	P	S	○	R
F	R	E	R	K	Q	N	I	T	X	C	T	L
A	T	L	○	N	T	A	U	O	E	U	M	A
V	B	N	N	R	W	S	T	D	O	V	U	D
C	N	Y	T	K	I	T	E	J	I	Y	S	A
A	H	E	D	O	A	D	G	W	P	E	I	F
L	N	R	L	M	S	P	B	M	P	L	J	N
F	Q	F	○	U	G	H	T	C	I	P	R	L
T	M	P	C	J	K	Q	W	Y	S	V	O	A
R	P	D	T	E	A	B	H	D	S	U	G	U
A	H	D	S	J	G	M	U	N	○	O	N	F
F	T	N	C	H	M	S	K	S	S	R	O	I
S	○	R	R	E	N	D	E	R	S	L	T	N
G	O	L	T	R	W	S	A	Y	I	Z	U	Y
P	S	F	L	E	H	N	L	O	M	T	C	I
D	O	B	V	K	R	U	P	V	G	J	S	M

(1861: Grant in charge of) **Union** (forces in parts of IL and MO)

(Grant trained the St.) **Louis** (militia)

(1861: Ft.) **Sumter** (was attacked)

(some Southern states) **seceded**

(Grant accepted only) **full** (surrender of enemies)

(Grant's nickname: "Unconditional) **Surrender** (Grant")

(did not) **swear**

(did not tell) **dirty** (stories)

(Grant's soldiers) **respected** (him)

(was promoted to) **Major** (General)

(1863: defeated the) **South** (at Vicksburg)

(he kept the) **Mississippi** (R. in Union hands)

(Gen. Grant pursued Gen.) **Lee**

(Gen. Sherman marched to) **Atlanta**

(Lee and Grant) **fought** (at the Battle of the Wilderness)

(Lee and) **Grant** (fought at Spotsylvania)

(Lee and Grant fought at North) **Anna** (R.)

(Lee and Grant fought at) **Cold** (Harbor)

(1865: Lee surrendered at) **Appomattox**

(1865: Grant let Lee's men take their) **guns** (home)

Ulysses S. Grant
1869–1877

SAME FIRST LETTER
DIRECTIONS
Find two words that begin with the same letter for each of these letters. The circled letter is the first letter for each answer.

Example:

(F) **O U R**
Grants had _____ children.

R E D E R I C K
one son's name

(T) _ _ _ _ _ _ _ _
Ku Klux Clan did this to black people.

_ _ _ _ _ _
Grant used these gov't forces to protect black people from the Ku Klux Klan.

(S) _ _ _ _ _
Grant tried to heal the anger in the North and _____.

_ _ _ _ _ _
This system gave jobs for election help.

(R) _ _ _ _ _ _
Grant worked to get these for blacks.

_ _ _ _
Klan members wore hoods and _____ to hide their identity and terrorize blacks.

(V) _ _ _ _ _
Grant ensured this right for black Americans.

_ _ _ _
Grant was a _____ honest man.

(D) _ _ _ _
Grant got the national _____ reduced.

_ _ _ _ _ _ _ _
There were scandals about _____ government men.

(E) _ _ _ _ _ _
The Grants visited this country.

_ _ _ _ _ _
The Grants visited this continent.

SCRAMBLED WORDS
DIRECTIONS
Unscramble the words and write the answers on the lines provided. (Use scrap paper to work out your answers.)

1. After retiring from the presidency, Grant took his wife and son, Jesse, to PUOERE. _____

2. Everywhere Grant's family traveled overseas, people EEHRCDE them. _____

3. A great crowd EOELWCMD them in San Francisco. _____

4. The Grants were honored with a EDAAPR in Chicago. _____

5. Grant bought a EOHM in WNE KYRO. _____ _____

6. Grant finished a OKBO about his EILF two days before he died of cancer. _____

Rutherford B. Hayes
1877–1881

CROSSWORD PUZZLE

ACROSS
1. 1853: The Rutherfords had a son, _____.
6. At 7, Rutherford (Ruddy) often visited the family _____. (house, barn, land)
7. Ruddy went to college at _____.
10. Father's name: _____
14. Fanny was Ruddy's older _____ and best friend.
15. 1860: Eleven states seceded from the _____.
18. 1860: Lincoln was elected _____.
19. Ruddy fell in love with _____ Webb.
20. He studied _____ in Columbus, Ohio. (profession)
21. Escaped _____ came through Cincinnati on the Underground Railroad.
25. Pres. Lincoln asked for _____ volunteers. (military)
26. Ruddy had the best grades in _____.
30. He joined the _____ army. (area)
31. Jefferson Davis was _____ president.

DOWN
2. Mother, Sophia, taught Ruddy to _____.
3. Ruddy: Appointed _____ in 23rd Infantry Regiment. (rank)
4. Fanny urged Ruddy to become someone _____. (special)
5. He became a _____ in Lower Sandusky, OH.
8. Father _____ before Ruddy's birth.
9. 1858: Ruddy Hayes became city _____. (occupation)
11. Birth state: _____
12. 1849: He moved to _____, a city near the Ohio R.
13. 1825: Ruddy's brother _____. (fatal accident)
16. 1852: Ruddy and Lucy were _____.
17. "Ruddy" was Rutherford Hayes's _____.
21. Mother's name: _____
22. Ruddy was wounded in battle in _____. (state)
23. His regiment fought in _____ Virginia.
24. Was friendly and _____ in school. (well-liked)
27. Civil War: Major _____ was known for bravery.
28. Ruddy could memorize and _____ patriots' speeches.
29. Father and _____: same first name

Rutherford B. Hayes
1877–1881

CROSSING OVER

DIRECTIONS
Use a pencil for this game. Find words from the following list that have the correct number of spaces and letters to fit into the crossing-over boxes (the words not in parentheses). Each word has a place where it belongs. The first word is done for you. To continue, find an eleven-letter word having an "a" in the third space. All the words tell about Rutherford B. Hayes.

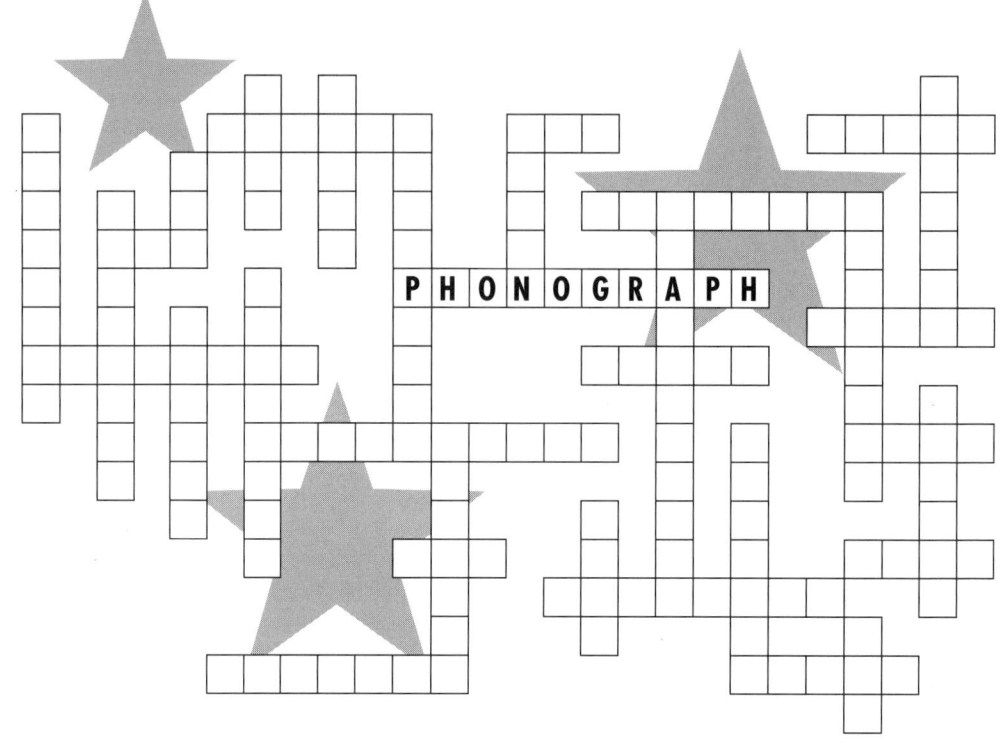

3 letters
(Ruddy: in Civil) **War**
(1865:) **Lee** (surrendered)
(The Hayes had) **one** (daughter)
(1877: Pullman railroad) **car** (invented)
son (Webb: his personal secretary)

4 letters
(someone) **shot** (a bullet into his house)
(Mrs. Hayes: nicknamed Lemonade) **Lucy** (for serving lemonade in Pres. House)
(1893: Ruddy Hayes) **died**
(lived in Fremont) **Ohio**

5 letters
(he was known for good) **sense**
(younger Hayes children had a) **black** (nanny)
(railroad problems) **ended**
(Hayes family sang by the) **piano**
seven (sons)
(1879: Edison invented) **light** (bulb)

6 letters
(Civil War: Ruddy got six) **bullet** (wounds)
(presidential election) **bitter**
(Hayes) **prayed** (each morning)

7 letters
(Lucy had) **college** (degree)

(1876:) **running** (water in Pres. House)
(Hayes tried) **mending** (the feelings between North and South)
(Hayes: made sure) **Indians** (were treated well)

8 letters
(future Pres.) **McKinley** (served in Hayes's regiment)
(Hayes's bravery encouraged) **soldiers**
(Hayes in U.S.) **Congress**
(1867:) **governor** (of OH)
(presidential election) **disputed**
(Hayes sent troops to stop railroad) **violence**
(Hayes allowed no alcoholic) **drinking** (in Pres. House)

9 letters
(1876: Bell invented) **telephone**

10 letters
(Helped found Ohio State) **University**
(Edison brought) **phonograph** (invention to Pres. House)

11 letters
(1877: Hayes) **inaugurated** (pres.)

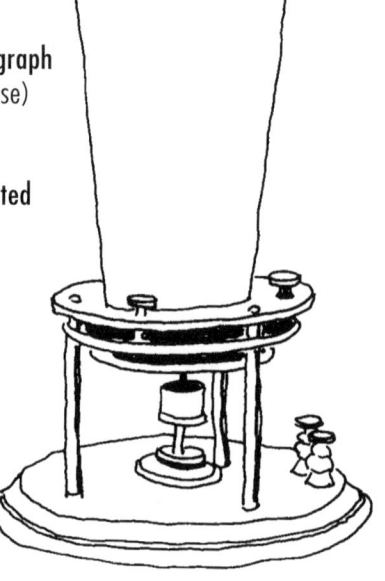

Rutherford B. Hayes
1877–1881

RUTHERFORD'S AND FANNY'S CHILDHOOD PAIRS
DIRECTIONS
All of Rutherford's and Fanny's childhood words in the large box are written twice, except for one. Write the name of each pair on a line. (Cross off the pairs as you find them.) Then find the name of the childhood word that appears only once, and write it in the box.

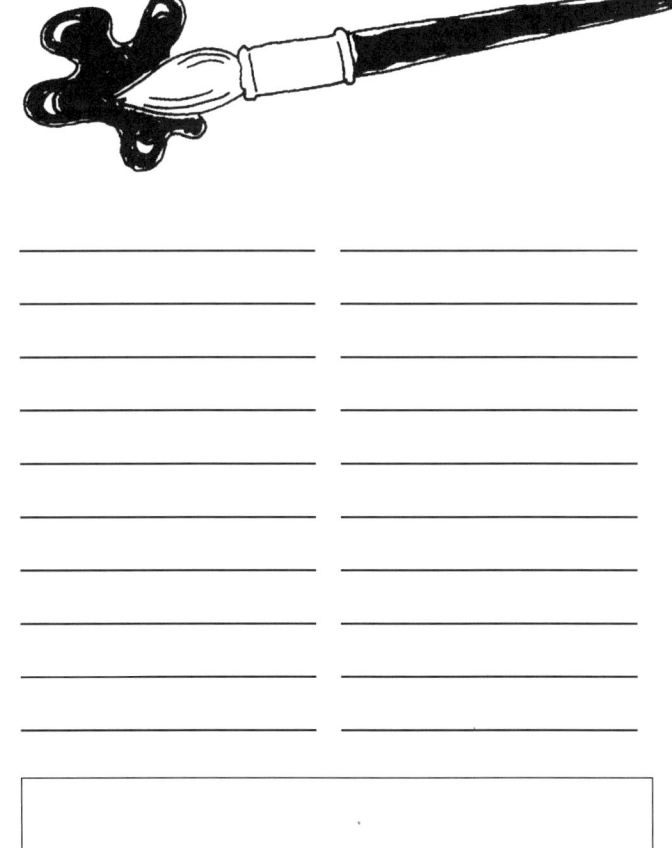

Words in the box: reading, writing, painting, spelling, games, farm, candy, minnows, tricks, affection, writing, stories, sports, hiding, fishing, farm, sports, rifle shooting, chess, stories, hiding, swimming, spelling, reading, painting, laughing, candy, brook, brook, laughing, baseball, minnows, fishing, swimming, ice skating, affection, ice skating, chess, rifle shooting, baseball

ALPHABET SEARCH
DIRECTIONS
Using words from any of the game pages about Hayes, find words that begin with these letters of the alphabet.

A _____   H _____   O _____
B _____   I _____   P _____
C _____   J _____   R _____
D _____   K _____   S _____
E _____   L _____   T _____
F _____   M _____   W _____
G _____   N _____   Y _____

57

James A. Garfield
1881

CROSSWORD PUZZLE

ACROSS

3. Birthplace: _____ of Cleveland, OH (direction)
4. James spoke strongly against _____. (bondage)
6. 1848: Got a job leading horses that pulled _____ along a canal.
8. He loved to _____ best of all. (devour printed words)
9. Went to school and got a _____ to teach. (paper)
10. Born in a log _____.
11. Father's name: _____

13. James: born _____ 19, 1831
16. At 3: Was carried 3 miles, to and from _____ by sister Hetty.
18. Was horrified to see so many men _____ in war.
20. Had _____ brothers and sisters.
21. 1860: Gave speeches to help _____ become president.
23. 1856: Graduated from college with _____ for good grades. (praise)
25. 1861: Lincoln tried to send food supplies to Ft. _____.
26. Southern states _____ from the Union.
27. The Garfields had a _____, Eliza.

DOWN

1. Wife's name: _____
2. 1858: James and Lucretia were _____. (wed)
5. He _____ to join the army.
7. He _____ to read at age 3 or 4.
12. 1858: At 26, James was _____ of Ohio's Hiram College. (top official)
14. Birth state: _____
15. James's mother gave a corner of her land for a local _____. (for learning)
17. 1859: James studied _____ on his own. (legal books)
19. At 28: Was elected to the Ohio _____.
22. 1861: Confederates _____ on Ft. Sumter.
24. Mother's name: _____

James A. Garfield
1881

WORD SEARCHING
DIRECTIONS
In the grid, find these words about James Garfield (the words that are not in parentheses). They can go up, down, across, at an angle, forward, or backward.

R	A	E	G	L	D	H	B	M	A	J	O	R
E	V	I	F	A	J	M	P	I	F	L	N	E
S	C	K	Q	R	U	W	Z	S	Y	A	V	I
P	O	T	K	E	N	T	U	C	K	Y	M	G
E	D	B	G	N	C	F	J	H	O	I	O	H
C	M	K	N	E	X	C	E	L	L	E	N	T
T	E	S	L	G	U	V	Y	A	T	P	E	R
E	W	H	B	D	E	D	N	E	C	D	Y	Z
D	E	O	G	I	F	K	S	J	B	L	W	H
O	M	U	S	S	E	R	G	N	O	C	S	P
R	B	S	U	Y	O	W	A	Z	R	T	C	V
F	I	E	E	H	M	K	S	J	N	L	Q	D
H	O	G	T	S	T	U	R	E	T	B	E	P
D	N	W	L	B	S	A	D	C	V	L	Z	Y
E	G	S	R	F	E	Y	P	H	K	A	O	M
I	J	A	Y	I	W	B	L	E	D	C	L	U
D	V	C	V	E	F	N	W	U	S	K	T	S

(his father) **died** (before James was 2)

(1861: Col. Garfield and troops drove Confederate forces from) **Kentucky**

(1862: elected to) **Congress** (while still in the army)

(promoted to Brig.) **General**

(1863: for bravery, was promoted to) **Major** (General)

(1863: his) **horse** (was shot from under him in battle)

(1863: son, Harry, was) **born**

(1863: at the Capitol, James was an) **excellent** (speaker)

(1865: Civil War) **ended**

(most) **slaves** (couldn't read or write)

(James wanted) **black** (people to have citizenship)

(1868:) **Ulysses** (Grant was president)

(1869: James bought a) **house** (in Washington)

(Garfield was elected to Congress) **eight** (times)

(1869: railroad finished from east to) **west**

(James, in charge of gov't) **money** (knew where it went)

(James was a very) **respected** (man)

(1874: the Garfields had) **five** (living children)

59

James A. Garfield
1881

CLUE
DIRECTIONS
Each set of lines has vowels and an occasional consonant to help you determine the correct answer. All the words tell about James A. Garfield.

1. The b u __ __ e __ in James's body couldn't be __ o u __ __.
2. September 1881: __ a __ __ i e __ d __ i e __.
3. Eliza, James's mother, died __ e __ e __ years after his __ e a __ __.
4. __ u __ __ e __ i a died in 1918.
5. James and his wife had seven __ __ i __ __ __ e __ in all.

NAME THE FARM
DIRECTIONS
Fill in the dotted lines with your answers. If they are correct, the circled letters will spell the name of the Garfields' farm.

1. James's mother, _____, attended his inauguration.
2. _____ people gained the right to vote.
3. Serious childhood disease: _____ cough
4. The Garfields bought a farm in _____, Ohio.
5. 1863: The Capitol's dome was not _____.
6. 1881: In a _____ station, Garfield was shot.
7. People had much _____ for Garfield. (high regard)
8. 1880: Garfield was _____ to the Senate.
9. 1881: Garfield was _____ president.

1. __ O __ __ __
2. __ __ O __ __
3. __ O __ __ __ __ __ __
4. __ __ O __ __ __ __
5. __ __ O __ __ __ __ __
6. __ __ O __ __
7. __ __ O __ __ __
8. __ __ O __ __ __ __
9. __ __ __ __ __ __ __ __ O

60

Chester A. Arthur
1881–1885

CROSSWORD PUZZLE

ACROSS

1. 1854: Chester became a _____. (occupation)
3. Birth state: _____
8. Carefully spent gov't _____ for war.
9. 1844: Arthurs _____ to Schenectady, NY.
12. Father was a Baptist _____. (occupation)
13. Had two boys; one _____.
15. Mother's name: _____
16. 1845: Chester entered _____. (advanced school)
17. Chester _____ law.
19. 1859: Chester and Ellen were _____. (wed)
21. Telegraph: between Chicago and New _____.
23. Chester practiced _____. (occupation)
24. 1885: *Huckleberry* _____ was published.
27. (1859) Chester, as quartermaster, used good _____. (sense)
28. Ellen's family lived in the _____. (Confederate part of U.S.)
29. After the Civil War, he returned to law _____.
31. He inspected _____ (military installations).
32. Used gov't money _____ for troops. (with wisdom)

DOWN

2. Chester met _____.
4. Born: _____ 1829
5. Many _____ came to the U.S. from other countries.
6. Earned $50,000 a year as custom's collector at _____ York Port.
7. 1861: Chester _____ everything he ordered. (as quartermaster)
10. Ancestors came from _____. (country)
11. Taught _____ to help pay college expenses.
14. 1848: War with _____ ended. (country)
18. Ellen's father, Capt. Herndon, _____ with his ship. (perished)
19. Chester found housing for NY _____. (army recruits)
20. Was very _____. (character trait)
22. Defended the _____ of blacks.
25. Inspected _____ he fed. (military)
26. Won court case for a black _____. (educator)
30. 1863: The Arthurs' _____ died. (child)

Chester A. Arthur
1881–1885

SUPPLY THE VOWEL
DIRECTIONS
In the grid, look for the following words (the words that are not in parentheses). The words can go up, down, across, at angles, backward, or forward. Parts of words may overlap. Supply the correct vowel—a e i o u—for the center of each word group.

(1839: father, William, moved his family to) **Union** (Valley, NY)

(many Northerners wanted to) **punish** (the South)

(Lincoln wanted the) **South** (to be treated kindly)

(the four time) **zones** (were created)

(Johnson wanted to follow Lincoln's) **plan** (for the South)

(1860s: Chester was) **customs** (collector for NY)

(Chester was an) **honest** (man)

taxes (were collected on goods coming through NY harbor)

(1864: the Arthurs had baby) **Alan**

Buffalo (Bill toured the U.S.)

(1865:) **Civil** (War ended)

(1865: after the Civil War) **ended** (Chester helped with war claims)

(1871: the Arthurs had a baby) **girl**

(Pres. Grant reduced Chester's salary to $12,000 as customs) **collector**

(Chester was against) **slavery**

(many Southerners were left) **homeless**

(1880) **Ellen** (became ill)

(1880: Ellen) **died**

(1881: Chester was elected) **vice**(-president)

(1882:) **Jesse** (James was killed)

A	D	B	L	D	E	H	C	A	G	P	G	F
V	E	R	J	N	D	K	T	L	L	O	T	I
C	O	V	I	L	E	S	L	O	V	E	R	Y
G	D	C	M	A	D	R	N	N	X	T	S	P
L	Y	A	E	J	N	B	W	C	V	E	D	U
F	C	O	L	L	E	C	T	O	R	T	S	E
I	H	K	G	L	M	S	H	N	J	S	P	O
Q	V	S	L	E	T	W	S	T	Y	E	A	Z
B	C	E	G	E	L	H	F	E	U	N	Z	D
R	N	M	J	S	S	E	L	E	M	O	H	I
H	L	Q	O	M	N	R	P	N	N	H	S	T
K	S	V	Y	O	U	E	O	E	C	S	B	R
Z	H	I	F	T	D	I	S	U	W	K	L	A
I	G	W	N	S	N	D	F	G	I	J	M	P
L	V	B	B	U	F	F	A	L	O	T	S	E
Y	P	M	Y	C	P	N	C	U	O	W	H	K
A	R	J	A	E	O	D	T	C	S	N	B	V

Chester A. Arthur
1881–1885

SKYSCRAPER
DIRECTIONS
Write your answers in the boxes. The circled letters will help you.

1. Abbr. for Vermont, Chester's birth state
2. He had _____ sisters. (number)
3. He had _____ brothers. (number)
4. His younger sister, _____, was his President's House hostess.
5. He installed indoor _____ in the President's House.
6. To ease going up and down steps, Chester had an _____ put in the President's House.
7. He _____ (restored) the run-down President's House. (later called the White House)
8. Ellen died of _____. (a lung disease)
9. 1881: Arthur was _____ president.
10. A German man discovered the germ that caused _____, a disease common in the 1700s and 1800s. (also called consumption)

NUMBER CODE
DIRECTIONS
Look at the numbers under each line. Find the matching numbers in the code box, and write the letters on the corresponding answer lines.

1. 1881: President Garfield was ___ ___ ___ ___ (19 8 15 20), and Arthur became ___ ___ ___ ___ ___ ___ ___ ___ (16 18 5 19 9 4 5 14 20).

2. ___ ___ ___ ___ (14 5 12 12), nine, and ___ ___ ___ ___ (1 12 1 14), sixteen, lived with their father in the President's House.

3. On vacations, Chester ___ ___ ___ ___ ___ (12 15 22 5 4) to ___ ___ ___ ___ (6 9 19 8).

4. 1882: Immigration was ___ ___ ___ ___ ___ ___ (12 9 13 9 20 5 4).

5. The law, in 1883: ___ ___ ___ ___ ___ (5 24 1 13 19) were required for ___ ___ ___ ___ ___ ___ ___ ___ ___ ___ ___ (7 15 22 5 18 14 13 5 14 20 10 15 2 19).

6. 1882: Arthur had a painful ___ ___ ___ ___ ___ ___ ___ ___ ___ ___ ___ ___ (11 9 4 14 5 25 19 9 3 11 14 5 19 19).

7. 1886: Arthur ___ ___ ___ ___ (4 9 5 4).

8. He was ___ ___ ___ ___ ___ ___ (2 21 18 9 5 4) in ___ ___ ___ ___ ___ ___ ___ (1 12 2 1 14 25), NY.

A - 1	N - 14
B - 2	O - 15
C - 3	P - 16
D - 4	Q - 17
E - 5	R - 18
F - 6	S - 19
G - 7	T - 20
H - 8	U - 21
I - 9	V - 22
J - 10	W - 23
K - 11	X - 24
L - 12	Y - 25
M - 13	Z - 26

63

Grover Cleveland
1885–1889

CROSSWORD PUZZLE

ACROSS

1. Grover's father was a _____. (spiritual occupation)
4. As a boy, Grover worked for Erie _____ shippers. (waterway)
6. He always worked _____. (diligently)
7. Born: _____ 18, 1837
8. Mother's name: _____
10. As a boy, he had good _____. (insight)
11. Had _____ brothers and sisters.
12. Father _____ in 1853. (Grover was 16.)
16. Father moved family to _____, NY. (Grover was 4.)
19. Grover believed time must not be _____. (unused)
21. A boyhood duty: pulling _____ (unwanted plants)
23. At school, he learned to _____.
24. 1861: Civil _____ began.
26. 1860: Buffalo had _____. (industrial buildings)
28. 1855: Grover visited his uncle in _____, NY.
29. In school, Grover learned to _____.
30. 1860: Many of _____ arrived in the U.S. daily.

DOWN

1. At 14, he earned _____ for his family.
2. Father's name: _____
3. Grover went to a _____ schoolhouse. (color)
4. Boyhood duty: _____ wood for the fireplace
5. Fayetteville: near the _____ Canal
6. Home: Taught to be _____. (character trait)
9. His full name: _____ Grover Cleveland.
13. Uncle Lewis got Grover a job with a Buffalo _____ firm.
14. Birthplace: Caldwell, New _____.
15. Grover read his _____ (holy book) and learned verses.
17. 1859: Grover became a _____ and sent money to help his mother.
18. Fayetteville was about eight miles from _____, NY.
20. He liked to fish and _____.
22. Southern planters had _____ to work hard.
25. Boyhood duty: watching _____ brothers and sisters (sibling rank)
27. Grover worked, sent money home; brothers joined the _____. (military)

64

Grover Cleveland
1885–1889

CROSSING OVER

DIRECTIONS

Use a pencil for this game. Using the words that are not in parentheses, find words from the following list that have the correct number of spaces and letters to fit into the crossing-over boxes. Each word has a place where it belongs. The first word is done for you. To continue, find a five-letter word having an "r" in the fourth space. All the words tell about Grover Cleveland.

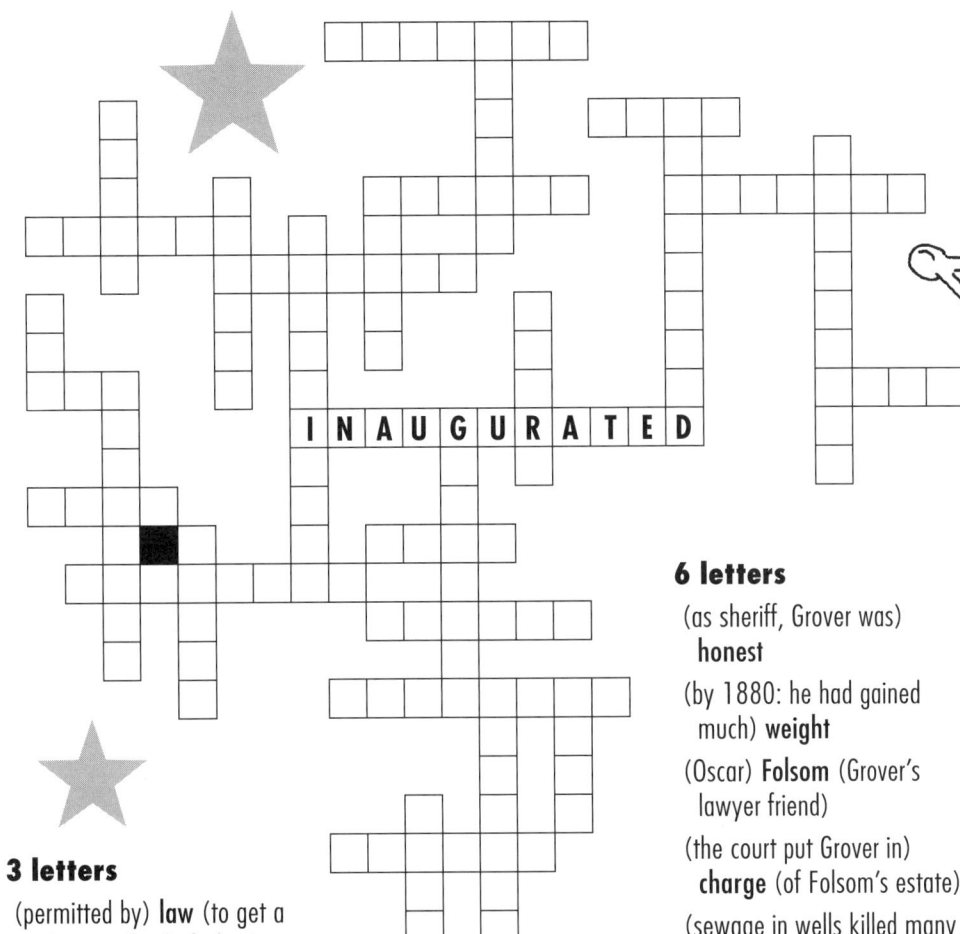

3 letters
(permitted by) **law** (to get a substitute for draft duty)
(April 9, 1865, Civil) **War** (ended)

4 letters
(Grover: drafted into the) **army**
(Buffalo: near the) **Erie** (Canal)
(1875: friend Oscar Folsom) **died**
(1882: Mayor Grover Cleveland said he'd fire employees who didn't) **work** (when they should)
(he was nicknamed "Grover the) **Good**(")

5 letters
(people sent faulty supplies to the jail, making Grover) **angry**
(Grover worked at a school for the) **blind**
(1882: Grover, 44, was elected) **mayor** (of Buffalo)
(wouldn't allow dishonesty in spending city) **money**
(hired good engineers so the poor got good) **water**

6 letters
(as sheriff, Grover was) **honest**
(by 1880: he had gained much) **weight**
(Oscar) **Folsom** (Grover's lawyer friend)
(the court put Grover in) **charge** (of Folsom's estate)
(sewage in wells killed many poor) **people**
(Grover: twenty-)**second** (president)

7 letters
(at 33, he was elected) **sheriff** (of Erie County)
(after people cheated on jail supplies, Grover) **counted** (all supplies)
(1864: Oscar Folsom's daughter) **Frances** (born)

8 letters
(Grover:) **attorney** (for Erie County, NY)
(he) **reported** (those who cheated on jail supplies)
(Grover: appointed) **guardian** (for Frances Folsom)
(1883: Grover) **governor** (of NY)

9 letters
(was well-known and) **respected**
(1881: Buffalo had) **dishonest** (leaders)

10 letters
(1882: attacking) **dishonesty** (in others, Grover saved Buffalo $1,000,000 before year's end)
(Grover: drafted, but got a) **substitute**

11 letters
(1885: Cleveland) **inaugurated** (president)

65

Grover Cleveland
1885–1889

SAME FIRST LETTER

DIRECTIONS

Find two words that begin with the same letter for each of these letters. The circled letter is the first letter for each answer.

Example:

(H)
H A R D
Grover worked ____.
H O M E
Grover sent money ____ to his mother.

(G) _ _ _ _ _ _ _ _ At Albany, he was ___ of New York.

_ _ _ _ Because he wouldn't give in to dishonest men, he was called "Grover the ___."

(F) _ _ _ _ _ _ Grover dealt ____ with the Indians.

_ _ _ _ _ _ _ Grover, 49, married ____ Folsom, 21.

(H) _ _ _ _ _ He worked many ___ each day.

_ _ _ _ _ _ _ Rose, Grover's sister, was ___ for the President's House.

(T) _ _ _ _ _ _ _ Before Rose came to Washington for her brother, she was a school ____.

_ _ _ _ _ _ _ Grover was the _____-second president.

(M) _ _ _ _ _ _ _ Grover was not ___ when he became president.

_ _ _ _ The government had much ____, so Grover lowered import taxes.

(W) _ _ _ _ _ _ _ Grover cut back the number of government ____.

_ _ _ _ _ Grover stood firm against government ____.

SCRAMBLED WORDS

DIRECTIONS

Unscramble the words and write the answers on the lines provided. (Use scrap paper to work out your answers.)

1. 1886: Grover and Frances Folsom were married in the LUBE MORO of the President's House. _____ _____
2. At the wedding, the Marine DABN played the wedding march. _____
3. Church LSBEL NARG after the wedding. _____ _____
4. After the wedding, 21 UGSN at the YVNA Yard fired in celebration. _____ _____
5. Grover and Frances spent time at his EOHUS in Georgetown, a section of Washington, D.C. _____
6. The Clevelands' house in Georgetown was called Oak WVIE. _____
7. Frances was hostess for receptions and ENIDNSR. _____
8. 1886: The ESTTAU of Liberty was dedicated by Grover. _____
9. 1889: The U.S. Dept. of Agriculture was created for SEAMFRR welfare. _____
10. Grover continued to stand firm against government EASWT. _____

66

Benjamin Harrison
1889–1893

CROSSWORD PUZZLE

ACROSS

4. Ben liked to _____, swim, and hunt.
7. From the farm, he saw _____ going down the Ohio R.
9. He was 7 when Grandfather William Henry Harrison was _____ pres.
10. Met Carrie Scott and fell in _____.
11. In _____, by the Ohio R., Ben studied law. (city)
15. 1841: Ben's grandfather, Pres. Harrison, was _____.
16. Ben's father hired a _____ for the farm's school. (instructor)
18. Birth state: North Bend, _____, 1833
19. Father, John, took harvest crops to New _____, LA.
20. Split-_____ piles were kept for fuel.
23. Favorite college subject: _____ (about the past)
24. Great-grandfather _____ the Declaration of Independence. (autographed)
25. 1854: Wife, Carrie, and Ben lived in _____, IN. (capital)
26. 1853: Ben and Carrie were _____.

DOWN

1. Indianapolis: Fish were _____ in the river.
2. Indianapolis: busy, industrial _____.
3. Ben started as a clerk announcing court _____. (proceedings)
4. Ben and Carrie lived at his father's _____ while he studied law. (house, barn, land)
5. A log school_____ was on the farm.
6. Ben liked to make the wax _____ for the table.
7. Most of their _____ was grown on the farm. (edible)
8. Indianapolis: Factories made _____ for clothes and things.
9. Mother's name: _____
12. Father's name: _____
13. A big _____ kept home and school warm.
14. Ben had _____ living sisters and brothers.
17. Ben's grandfather, Pres. Harrison, lived only one _____ after inauguration.
21. Ben graduated from _____. (higher learning)
22. 1850: Ben's mother and two of her children _____.

Benjamin Harrison
1889–1893

WORD SEARCHING
DIRECTIONS
In the grid, find these words about Benjamin Harrison (the words that are not in parentheses). They can go up, down, across, at an angle, forward, or backward.

(born) **August** (20, 1833)

(1850: North and South argued over) **slavery**

(1850: he went to Miami) **University** (Oxford, OH)

(1854: Ben became a) **lawyer**

(son) **Russell** (born, 1854)

(1855: Ben became a law) **partner** (with the governor's son)

(Ben: elected city) **attorney** (in Indianapolis)

(1858: daughter) **Mary** (born)

(Ben bought a two-story) **house** (for his family)

(1858: he) **enlisted** (in the army)

(was made a colonel in the) **army**

(before going to war: made sure his law partners would) **help** (his family)

(Ben's regiment guarded northern trains and tracks from the) **enemy**

(1864: the North was not winning the) **war**

(1864: Ben's regiment fought with Gen.) **Sherman** (in the South)

(Ben fought bravely with his) **men**

(regiment fought many fierce) **battles** (in GA)

(Ben and men marched into) **Atlanta** (with Sherman)

(escaped) **black** (slaves helped the Union Army)

A	C	U	B	E	D	B	L	A	C	K	G	H
I	K	L	N	P	O	M	N	R	Q	T	V	R
W	A	R	A	I	E	C	B	H	O	U	S	E
J	F	E	D	H	V	I	G	S	Y	Z	W	N
L	K	Y	Q	O	N	E	J	U	M	P	J	T
R	I	W	T	W	S	V	R	D	C	A	Y	R
H	Y	A	R	M	Y	U	T	S	U	G	U	A
G	R	L	F	J	S	M	B	K	I	L	E	P
O	E	P	N	S	R	Q	S	Y	E	T	V	U
X	V	W	E	A	T	T	O	R	N	E	Y	F
Z	A	L	N	Y	A	B	D	A	L	A	E	C
K	L	I	E	H	T	G	J	M	I	W	U	R
M	S	P	M	L	N	O	N	Q	S	V	Y	T
D	M	E	Y	A	A	B	A	T	T	L	E	S
O	Q	G	L	F	L	M	I	H	E	L	P	T
B	S	P	N	C	T	E	K	J	D	U	V	W
S	H	E	R	M	A	N	H	R	B	C	Y	A

Benjamin Harrison
1889–1893

SKYSCRAPER
DIRECTIONS
Write your answers in the boxes. The circled letters will help you.

1. Abbr. for Ben's home state
2. Ben was called home from the _____ to make speeches for the reelection of Lincoln.
3. 1864: Made speeches for more men to join the _____.
4. 1880: Nominated for U.S. _____.
5. 1884: Ben wanted higher _____. (taxes on imports)
6. 1889: Ben was inaugurated _____.
7. Gov't spending for pensions rose $135 million dollars per year; money was taken from the U.S. _____. (gov't bank)
8. Unwise gov't spending, minting of silver, and a drop in gold reserves led to a _____. (failing banks, job losses)
9. 1892: Wife, Carrie, died of _____.
10. 1892: Ben was defeated for _____. (another term)

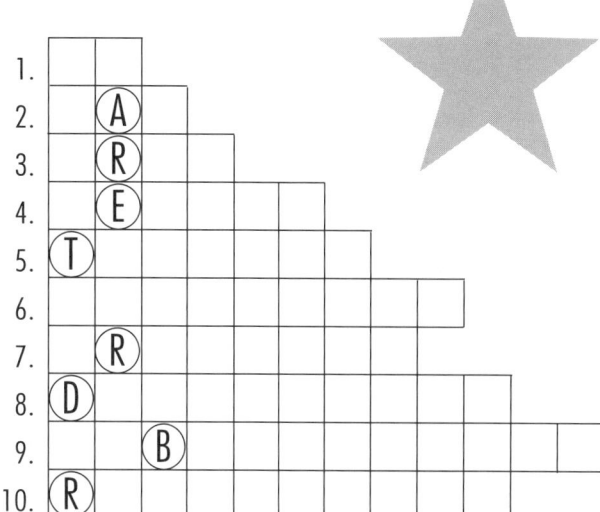

PAIRS
DIRECTIONS
All the Benjamin Harrison words in the large box are written twice, except for one. Write each Harrison pair on a line. (Cross off the pairs as you find them.) Find the name that appears only once, and write it in the box.

Grover Cleveland
2nd Term 1893–1897

CROSSWORD PUZZLE

ACROSS

1. First term: much _____ in U.S. Treasury
5. 1889: Pres. Harrison's Congress raised tariffs _____. (even more)
6. Grover wanted lower _____ on imports.
8. 1891: Baby _____ was born.
9. 1889: Unwise spending in Harrison's term nearly _____ the Treasury.
13. People loved to _____ about baby Ruth.
14. 1889: _____ was inaugurated president.
16. A severe _____ storm fell at his inauguration.
17. The poor began to _____ for better wages. (revolt)
19. He wanted money spent _____. (carefully)
20. Grover's mouth: severe _____
22. There were _____ and riots by poor workers.
24. Businesses went _____. (failed)
25. People wanted Grover to _____ jobs. (make)
26. Gov't _____ was at a low level. (precious metal)
27. 1893: People _____ their jobs.

DOWN

2. A doctor was asked to secretly _____ on Grover's mouth.
3. Harrison's Congress was called the "_____ Dollar Congress."
4. 1892: People wanted _____ to be pres. again.
7. Congress wanted money for unwise _____.
10. High tariffs on imports made industry owners rich; workers _____ and overworked.
11. 1892: America faced economic _____. (ruin)
12. The depression grew _____.
15. Too many _____ coins were made. (a lesser precious metal)
18. 1893: Grover was _____ pres. again.
19. Newspapers liked to _____ about baby Ruth.
21. The spot in Grover's mouth was _____. (disease)
23. He kept his operation a _____.
24. The operation was done on a _____. (vessel)

70

Grover Cleveland
2nd Term 1893–1897

SUPPLY THE VOWEL

DIRECTIONS

In the grid, look for the following words (the words that are not in parentheses). The words can go up, down, across, at angles, backward, or forward. Parts of words may overlap. Supply the correct vowel—a e i o u—for the center of each word group.

A	G	I	F	B	J	M	C	H	L	D	K	E
N	O	Q	U	T	N	V	R	Y	R	S	R	P
F	R	N	S	E	C	D	S	○	C	O	N	D
S	Y	○	B	A	T	G	Y	N	H	I	Y	W
B	L	I	B	J	M	W	P	O	R	T	N	K
T	V	R	S	Y	A	B	A	M	F	C	S	A
U	H	A	G	L	L	E	J	Y	M	V	I	E
L	U	M	W	T	O	S	W	F	G	F	D	H
R	G	D	B	D	R	A	H	C	○	R	A	O
C	P	K	N	I	L	O	Q	S	R	V	H	K
P	E	T	V	Y	F	S	H	A	L	C	E	R
E	U	S	H	O	D	J	W	J	S	B	M	G
M	H	T	○	R	I	H	L	N	H	B	R	O
E	G	R	N	O	F	S	I	C	N	○	R	F
R	T	F	G	W	H	N	H	K	Y	N	R	T
H	A	Y	R	U	K	V	S	B	R	K	E	D
I	L	T	Y	D	M	J	F	P	N	S	C	G

(many people were) **hungry**

(Grover was a) **lawyer**

(he loved to) **fish**

Gray (Gables was his summer home)

(summer) **house** (was in MA)

(people) **lost** (their jobs)

(daughter) **Marion** (born)

(Grover worked) **hard**

(son) **Richard** (born)

(many banks had no) **money**

(three) **girls**

(two) **boys**

(Grover's) **second** (term)

(2nd term: he was twenty-) **fourth** (pres.)

(son) **Francis** (born)

(daughter) **Esther** (born)

(many) **banks** (failed)

five (children)

Ruth (oldest child)

(Esther) **born** (in the President's House)

71

Grover Cleveland
2nd Term 1893–1897

NAME GROVER'S SUMMER HOME LOCATION

DIRECTIONS

Fill in the dotted lines with your answers. If they are correct, the circled letters will spell the place where Grover Cleveland had his summer home.

1. Ruth was the Clevelands' first _____.
2. 1886: Grover dedicated the _____ of Liberty.
3. The four time _____ were established across the United States.
4. There were no _____ codes for sending letters.
5. Grover refused to _____ the government's money.
6. 1889: The U.S. Dept. of Agriculture was created for _____ welfare.
7. 1893: Grover was inaugurated president for the _____ time.
8. Unwise spending by the Harrison administration brought on a serious _____.
9. Grover tried to solve the country's _____.
10. Ruth, 12, died of a serious disease, _____.
11. 1897: Grover took his family to Princeton, New _____, to live.
12. At 71, Grover had health _____.
13. In 1908, Grover grew very _____ and died.

ALPHABET SEARCH

DIRECTIONS

Using words from any of the game pages about Grover Cleveland, find words that begin with each letter of the alphabet. Try to find words in which alphabet letters are used only once in each word.

Example: Frances (Each letter is used once in the word.)

A _____   G _____   M _____   T _____
B _____   H _____   N _____   W _____
C _____   I _____   O _____   Y _____
D _____   J _____   P _____
E _____   K _____   R _____
F _____   L _____   S _____

72

William McKinley
1897–1901

23. A soldier on guard duty mistook a skunk for the _____; it smelled awful.
26. 1860: Abraham _____ was elected pres.
27. At Poland Academy, William studied _____. (diligently)
28. William drove mules to take _____ and water to troops.
29. Boyhood: His family _____ to Poland, OH.

DOWN

2. He and others discussed _____. (a divisive issue)
3. Lt. Col. Rutherford Hayes was impressed with _____. (first name)
4. As a boy he played _____ with a wooden sword. (combat)
5. 1861: The 23rd Regiment caused the _____ to retreat. (South)
6. He went to a one-room _____.
8. He taught school to help his _____.
11. Father managed an _____ foundry. (heavy metal)
12. Battle of Carnifex Ferry: The Union drove the _____ away.
14. Mother's name: _____
15. He worked at Poland Post _____. (mail)
19. As a student, he _____ all the time. (learned)
22. Boyhood: Chopped _____. (for fireplace)
24. Boyhood: Played _____. (ground game)
25. 1861: He joined the 23rd _____ Regiment. (foot soldiers)

CROSSWORD PUZZLE
ACROSS

1. William bravely _____ a Union regiment.
6. Ancestors: from _____.
7. Had _____ brothers and sisters.
9. 1862: 23rd Regiment joined the _____ of the Potomac.
10. Birthplace: Niles, _____.
13. Was quiet and liked to _____ to others talk. (hear)
16. Born: _____ 29, 1843
17. Ft. Sumter was _____ on by Confederates.
18. Boyhood: Liked to fly a _____.
19. Mother, Nancy helped the _____ and poor. (ailing)
20. As a teacher, he walked three _____ to and from school.
21. Boyhood: Drove _____ to pasture.

William McKinley
1897–1901

CROSSING OVER

DIRECTIONS
Use a pencil for this game. Find words from the following list that have the correct number of spaces and letters to fit into the crossing-over boxes (the words not in parentheses). Each word has a place where it belongs. The first word is done for you. To continue, find a twelve-letter word with "t" in the ninth space. All the words tell about William McKinley.

3 letters
(opened) **law** (office: Canton, OH)
(1869: met) **Ida** (Saxton)
(Ida became) **ill** (after her mother's death)
(tariff) **tax** (on imports)

4 letters
(wedding) **gift** (a house from her father)
(studied so hard he got) **sick**
(U.S. sent troops to) **Cuba**
fair (and courteous in law trials)
(fell in) **love** (with Ida)
(Spanish) **sank** (battleship *Maine*)
(Katherine died at age) **four**

5 letters
(battleship) *Maine* (was sent to Cuba)
(U.S. waged war against) **Spain**
(Perry sank Spanish) **ships** (in the Philippines)
(Roosevelt's) **Rough** (Riders captured San Juan Hill)

6 letters
(1866: went to law) **school**
(U.S.) **states** (from Atlantic to Pacific)
(1873) **second** (baby died)

7 letters
(at 17, William went to) **college**
(honored for) **bravery**
(William and Ida were) **married**
(William wanted high) **tariffs**
(knew how to make) **friends**
(an excellent) **speaker**
(was) **devoted** (to Ida)
(Cubans rebelled against) **Spanish** (rule)

8 letters
(William was sent to) **Congress**
(Became) **governor** (OH)

(Spanish army) **tortured** (Cubans)
(Gold: important for) **treasury**

9 letters
(baby) **Katherine** (born)
(passed laws for safer) **factories**
(Hawaii was made a U.S.) **territory**
(U.S.) **blockaded** (Spanish ships at Cuba)

10 letters
(Ida suffered from) **depression**

12 letters
(wife and his mother attended) **inauguration**

74

William McKinley
1897–1901

NUMBER CODE

DIRECTIONS
Look at the numbers under each line. Find the matching numbers in the code box, and write the letters on the corresponding answer lines.

A - 1	N - 14
B - 2	O - 15
C - 3	P - 16
D - 4	Q - 17
E - 5	R - 18
F - 6	S - 19
G - 7	T - 20
H - 8	U - 21
I - 9	V - 22
J - 10	W - 23
K - 11	X - 24
L - 12	Y - 25
M - 13	Z - 26

1. 1898: The U.S. Navy ___ ___ ___ ___ all Spanish ___ ___ ___ ___ ___ ___ at ___ ___ ___ ___.
   19 1 14 11   19 8 9 16 19   3 21 2 1

2. 1898: The U.S. captured ___ ___ ___ ___ ___ ___ ___ ___ ___ ___.
   16 21 5 18 20 15 18 9 3 15

3. A peace treaty with Spain gave the island of ___ ___ ___ ___ and
   7 21 1 13

   the ___ ___ ___ ___ ___ ___ ___ ___ ___ ___ to the U.S.
   16 8 9 12 9 16 16 9 14 5 19

4. William Howard Taft was appointed Civil ___ ___ ___ ___ ___ ___ ___ ___ of the Philippines.
   7 15 22 5 18 14 15 18

5. 1898: ___ ___ ___ ___ ___ was open to Western ___ ___ ___ ___ ___.
   3 8 9 14 1   20 18 1 4 5

6. Col. Theodore Roosevelt was elected N.Y. ___ ___ ___ ___ ___ ___ ___ ___.
   7 15 22 5 18 14 15 18

7. McKinley was ___ ___ ___ ___ ___ ___ ___ ___ ___ ___ ___ ___ ___ ___.
   9 14 1 21 7 21 18 1 20 5 4 1 7 1 9 14

8. 1901: William and Ida took a ___ ___ ___ ___ ___ ___ ___ ___ ___ across the U.S.
   20 18 1 9 14   20 18 9 16

9. September 1901: William and Ida went to the ___ ___ ___ ___ ___ ___ ___ ___ ___ ___
   16 1 14 1 13 5 18 9 3 1 14

   ___ ___ ___ ___ ___ ___ ___ ___ ___ ___ in Buffalo, NY.
   5 24 16 15 19 9 20 9 15 14

10. People came to ___ ___ ___ ___ ___ the president in the large ___ ___ ___ ___ ___ ___ of ___ ___ ___ ___ ___ at the
    7 18 5 5 20   20 5 13 16 12 5   13 21 19 9 3

    Exposition.

11. At the Exposition, Pres. McKinley ___ ___ ___ ___ ___ ___ ___.
    23 1 19   19 8 15 20

12. He ___ ___ ___ ___ on September 13, 1901.
    4 9 5 4

13. Vice-President ___ ___ ___ ___ ___ ___ ___ ___ ___ ___ ___ ___ ___ ___ ___ ___ ___
    20 8 5 15 4 15 18 5   18 15 15 19 5 22 5 12 20

    was inaugurated the ___ ___ ___ ___ ___ ___ – ___ ___ ___ ___ ___ president of the U.S.
                       20 23 5 14 20 25   19 9 24 20 8

14. The ___ ___ ___ ___ ___ ___ ___ died in the ___ ___ ___ ___ ___ ___ ___ ___ ___ ___ ___ ___ ___.
        1 19 19 1 19 19 9 14   5 12 5 3 20 18 9 3   3 8 1 9 18

15. McKinley was buried in ___ ___ ___ ___ ___ ___, OH.
    3 1 14 20 15 14

75

Theodore Roosevelt
1901–1909

CROSSWORD PUZZLE

ACROSS

3. Teddy shot a _____ bear. (fierce)
4. He bought a cattle _____ out west.
5. His ancestors were from _____. (country)
9. 1886: Teddy married Edith in London, _____. (country)
10. Elected to NY Legislature in _____, NY.
12. Mother's name: _____
15. Home-schooled by _____. (teachers)
16. Father imported plate _____. (transparent)
17. Later, Teddy met _____ Carow, a childhood friend.
18. Mother had _____ children besides Teddy.
20. He could shoot and _____ birds. (taxidermy)
21. Father's name was the _____ as Theodore's.
22. Teddy collected bones, rocks, and _____. (four-footed creatures)
25. Teddy's sister, _____, took care of baby Alice.
26. Teddy's first wife, Alice, _____ two days after baby Alice's birth.
27. 1878: Teddy met Alice Lee and fell in _____.
28. Teddy: Born _____ 27, 1858.
29. 1891: Baby _____ born to Edith.

DOWN

1. 1884: Baby Alice was _____ to wife, Alice.
2. As a child, he was thin, weak and _____. (ill)
3. Mother, Martha: born in _____. (state)
6. Learned naval _____ from Confederate uncles. (fighting)
7. 1880: Teddy and Alice were _____. (wed)
8. He pursued _____. (sport using fists)
11. During the Civil War, Father was for the North; Martha for the _____.
13. Father had much money and a fine _____.
14. Teddy: serious breathing disease called _____.
19. Father bought Teddy gym _____ for exercising.
20. Teddy watched _____ animals. (size)
21. With relentless exercise, he became _____.
23. His eyesight was very _____. (weak)
24. While pres., he insisted on _____ for gov't job seekers. (exams)
25. Teddy, second wife Edith, and little _____ lived in NY. (his first child)

Presidential Puzzlers Copyright © 2005 Good Year Books

Theodore Roosevelt
1901–1909

WORD SEARCHING
DIRECTIONS
In the grid, find these words about Theodore Roosevelt (the words that are not in parentheses). They can go up, down, across, at an angle, forward, or backward.

S	F	H	C	G	M	A	I	N	E	B	D	A
H	D	N	I	T	O	L	U	O	C	L	K	J
O	M	H	S	E	Y	V	W	P	A	T	U	P
T	A	G	R	C	G	I	E	B	D	Q	B	R
E	W	U	K	Q	T	M	I	R	O	L	J	E
G	B	O	O	K	S	H	S	U	N	W	R	S
N	A	R	H	E	C	T	C	P	S	O	Y	I
I	G	C	E	R	O	D	O	E	H	T	R	D
F	N	L	A	M	J	F	R	I	I	Q	V	E
Y	T	H	S	I	B	S	R	K	P	I	O	N
Q	V	P	W	T	U	E	U	L	S	J	K	T
U	D	E	C	B	H	K	P	R	V	I	C	E
E	G	L	G	Y	A	T	T	A	C	K	R	S
N	F	Y	U	M	W	P	I	R	D	N	U	F
T	L	H	H	Y	A	P	O	L	I	C	E	P
I	I	T	M	Y	V	A	N	C	D	B	L	G
N	N	E	X	C	E	L	L	E	N	T	E	O

(Teddy attacked) **corruption** (wherever he found it)

(he attacked) **police** (corruption)

(1887: baby) **Theodore** (born)

(1889: baby) **Kermit** (born)

(1891: baby) **Ethyl** (born)

(1894: baby) **Archibald** (born)

(1895: Cubans rebelled against Spanish) **rule**

(the Spanish were) **cruel** (to Cubans)

(the Spanish in Cuba destroyed the U.S. ship) *Maine*

(Roosevelt and his) **Rough** (Riders went to Cuba)

(U.S. sank Spanish) **ships** (at Cuba)

(1897: baby) **Quentin** (born)

(1897: Teddy became ass't secretary of) **navy**

(he wrote many) **books**

(1899: Teddy was elected) **governor** (of NY)

(1901: McKinley was pres.; Roosevelt) **vice** (-pres.)

(1901: McKinley was) **shot**

(1901: Teddy became) **president**

(Teddy's children playfully planned an) **attack** (on him; Teddy jokingly sent them an official warning from the U.S. War Dept.)

(Teddy took up judo and was) **excellent** (at it)

Theodore Roosevelt
1901–1909

SCRAMBLED WORDS
DIRECTIONS
Unscramble the words and write the answers on the lines provided. (Use scrap paper to work out your answers.)

1. Teddy had two sisters and one brother. The name of one sister was NNAA and the name of the other sister was ROCNEIN. _____ _____

2. He earned fame for using CATT and diplomacy in averting war with other countries. _____

3. Teddy gave the official title of "IHWET SOHEU" to the President's House. _____ _____

4. 1904: The U.S. began digging the AAAPNM LNCAA. _____ _____

5. 1905: Teddy was inaugurated U.S. president NAIAG. _____

6. Army Doctor Gorgas rid Panama of LEYWLO VEFRE and cut malaria cases by 90 percent. _____ _____

7. 1914: The Canal was DELMTECPO. _____

CLUE
DIRECTIONS
Each set of lines has vowels and consonants to help you determine the correct answer. All the words tell about Theodore Roosevelt.

1. As president, Teddy worked very   __ a __ __.
2. He fought big   b u __ i __ e __ __   to help farmers and laborers.
3. Daughter Alice was   __ a __ __ i e __   in the White House. (wed)
4. Teddy was awarded the   __ o __ e __   __ e a __ e   Prize for keeping peace with other countries.
5. Teddy saved a bear cub's life, so stuffed   __ e a __ __   were sold and given the nickname of
   T e __ __ __   __ e a __ __.
6. Teddy insisted on   c a __ a __ __ e   men to serve as public officials.
7. Milwaukee: Roosevelt was shot, but not killed, by an   i __ __ a __ e   man.
8. 1914: The First   __ o __ __ d   __ a __   began.
9. Son, Quentin, was   __ i __ __ e __   in the war.
10. 1919: Teddy   __ i e __   of a   __ __ o o __   __ __ o __   in his heart.
11. Teddy's face, with three other presidents' faces, were   __ a __ __ e d   in stone on Mt. Rushmore.

William H. Taft
1909–1913

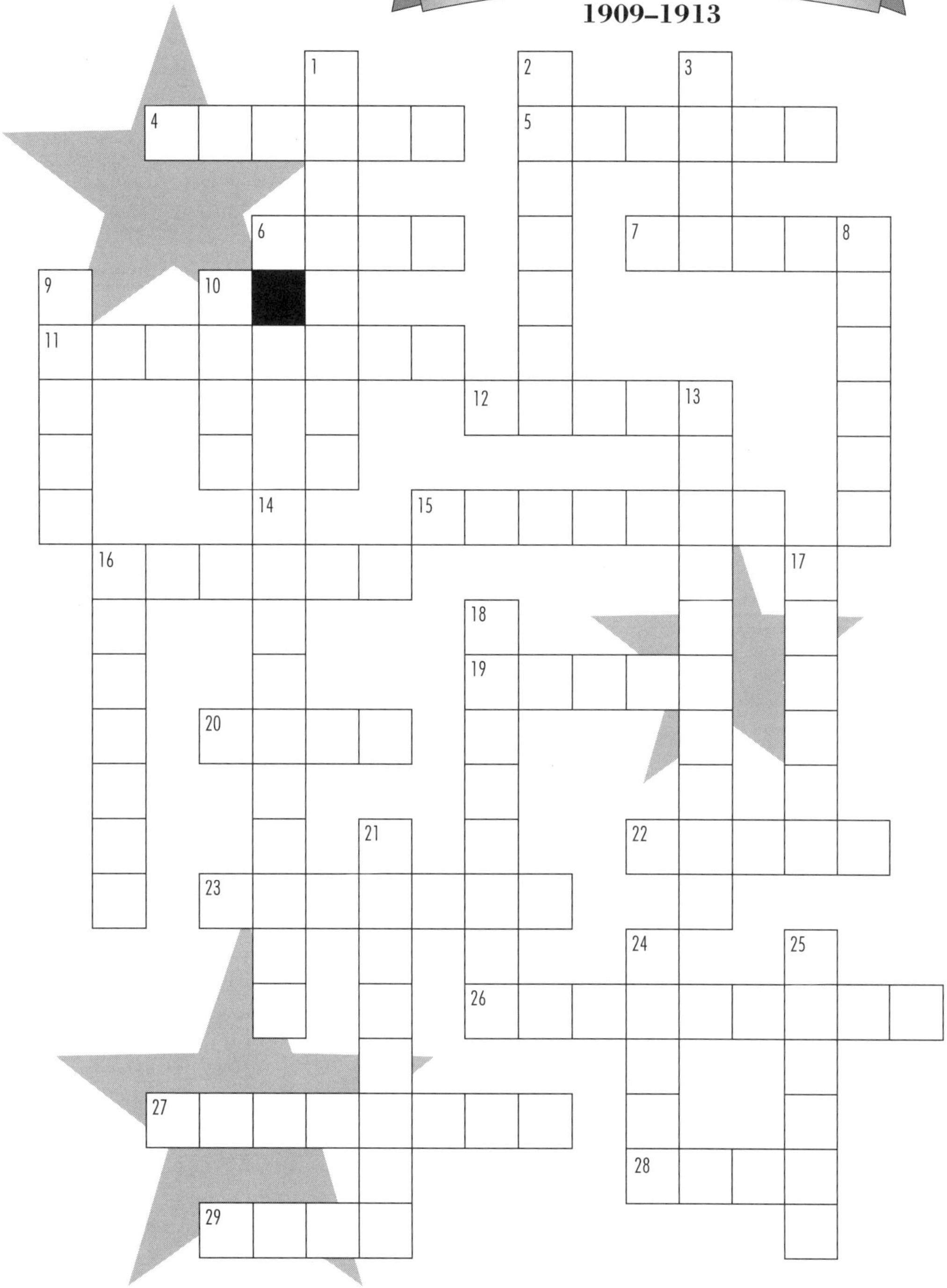

CROSSWORD PUZZLE

ACROSS

4. 1878: William went to law _____. (place to learn)
5. He recommended Goethals for chief engineer of the _____ Canal.
6. Was court reporter for a _____ paper.
7. The Tafts' daughter, _____, was born.
11. Father's name: _____
12. The Tafts had _____ children. (number)
15. The _____ made William sick. (equatorial zone)
16. Mother's name: _____
19. _____ boats passed Cincinnati.
20. 1891: His father _____.
22. Dr. Gorgas said mosquitoes cause yellow _____.
23. 1886: William and Nellie were _____. (wed)
26. 1905: He was appointed _____ of war by Teddy Roosevelt.
27. He solved _____ in other countries. (troubles)
28. Taft was _____ to the Filipinos. (tender-hearted)
29. He worked _____. (diligently)

DOWN

1. 1901: William became Civil _____ of the Philippines. (chief ruler)
2. 1900: U.S. annexed the Philippines after the _____-American War.
3. He attended _____ University in CT.
8. William met Helen, who was called _____.
9. Taft: very _____ as a judge (joyful)
10. 1888: Was appointed to the _____ Superior Court. (state)
13. Nellie _____ William to succeed. (urged)
14. Birthplace: _____, OH
16. He _____ all he could about the Philippines. (gathered information)
17. He liked the Filipino _____. (residents)
18. Had two _____ and one sister.
21. He _____ (toured) much in the Philippines.
24. He didn't smoke or _____.
25. The Tafts' summer home: Murray Bay, _____. (country)

William H. Taft
1909–1913

SUPPLY THE VOWEL

DIRECTIONS

In the grid, look for the following words (the words that are not in parentheses). The words can go up, down, across, at angles, backward, or forward. Parts of words may overlap. Supply the correct vowel—a e i o u—for the center of each word group.

- (Dr.) **Gorgas** (said mosquitoes cause yellow fever)
- (had concern for) **child** (labor)
- (birth state) **Ohio**
- (Taft solved problems within) **Cuba**
- (on certain products, he wanted) **free** (trade with Canada)
- (1906: Cuban) **rebels** (didn't want the U.S. there)
- (Taft made business leaders) **angry**
- (he made some) **wise** (choices for gov't)
- (had some problems being a) **leader**
- (fearful of rebels, the Cuban pres. wanted the United States to) **rule**
- (1909: Nellie had a) **stroke**
- (Taft was always) **fair** (in legal decisions)
- (was very) **honest**
- (had problems making) **decisions**
- (Taft got) **benefits** (for workers)
- (promoted safety for) **mine** (workers)
- (Taft didn't want to) **run** (for pres.)
- (laws passed for railroad workers') **safety**
- (was temporary) **governor** (of Cuba)
- (1909: was) **inaugurated** (U.S. president)

G	B	H	C	I	E	N	F	O	Q	K	L	J
D	A	M	H	S	O	R	P	S	I	U	E	M
D	E	C	○	S	I	O	N	S	V	H	K	H
W	Y	W	L	N	R	O	N	R	E	V	○	G
E	H	G	D	A	E	C	I	F	B	N	R	T
S	K	M	J	R	P	S	U	O	E	W	T	N
D	L	A	C	E	Y	Z	L	S	T	D	S	V
B	I	E	H	D	J	T	T	G	E	E	R	L
D	O	P	B	A	E	N	D	U	F	T	C	K
R	B	E	N	○	F	I	T	S	M	A	S	B
Y	G	V	R	L	R	T	I	Y	O	R	H	N
A	R	F	E	P	L	A	T	H	R	U	K	E
W	V	G	B	M	G	E	S	F	C	G	L	J
F	C	E	N	F	F	W	T	Y	R	○	N	I
G	O	R	G	○	S	R	B	N	R	A	B	E
K	V	U	S	I	C	M	J	H	W	N	O	A
T	L	D	D	R	S	I	A	U	F	I	P	G

80

William H. Taft
1909–1913

SAME FIRST LETTER
DIRECTIONS
Find two words that begin with the same letter for each of these letters. The circled letter is the first letter for each answer.

Example:

C. U B A
where the "Rough Riders" went

H I L D
Taft was concerned about _____ labor.

B __ __
____ Scouts of America were founded in 1910.

__ __
Taft was a ___ man, weighing 300 pounds at one time.

A __ __ __ __ __ __ __ __ __ __
Improvements were made in these family vehicles.

__ __ __
Taft was a college professor _____ he retired as president.

T __ __ __ __ __ __
big cruise ship that sank in 1912

__ __ __ __ __ __ __
Taft was _____ governor of Cuba.

P __ __ __
Admiral Perry and his friend reached the North ____.

__ __ __ __ __ __ __ __ __
Taft disliked his job as ____.

S __ __ __ __ __ __
The Girl ____ of America were founded in 1912.

__ __ __ __ __
Nellie had a _____, but got better.

R __ __ __ __ __ __ __
oldest son of the Tafts

__ __ __ __ __ __ __ __ __ __
political party Taft represented

SKYSCRAPER
DIRECTIONS
Write your answers in the boxes. The circled letters will help you.

1. Abbr. for Ohio
2. Taft wanted countries to get together and discuss problems before going to _____. (conflict)
3. He wanted _____ control in all countries. (weapons)
4. Many young children worked long _____ in factories.
5. Often young boys worked in factories late at _____.
6. Children worked in coal _____.
7. 1913: _____ was inaugurated president.
8. After his presidency, Taft became a professor at _____ University in CT.
9. At Yale, Nellie could talk again after her _____. (paralyzing illness)
10. Taft did much to help working _____.
11. 1921: Taft's lifelong dream came true when he became chief justice of the _____ Court.
12. 1930: He died at age _____-two.

Woodrow Wilson
1913–1921

CROSSWORD PUZZLE

ACROSS

2. He was _____ to others with less abilities.
7. Ancestry: Scotch-_____
10. Born _____ 29, 1856.
12. 1883: Met Ellen Axson and fell in _____.
13. As a boy he organized friends into groups and led them by using _____. (laws)
14. Father: Presbyterian _____
18. In college, he learned to _____ well.
20. Was well-_____.
22. Ellen and Woodrow were _____. (wed)
23. Woodrow persuaded Congress to lower _____. (import taxes)
26. First baby, _____, born.
27. Wilson family moved to _____. (state)
29. Gave _____ around the U.S. (talks)
30. Wilson sent _____ to Mexico. (military)
31. U.S. wanted to stay _____ in Europe's war. (separate)

DOWN

1. Father, Joseph, cared for wounded Confederate _____ in his church.
3. Wilson loved being on the _____ team at college. (argues)
4. Birth state: _____
5. 1861: _____ War began.
6. He was _____ by students at Princeton. (highly regarded)
8. Worked _____ in school. (diligently)
9. 1885: He taught _____ in college.
11. Father's name: _____
15. Wilson worked so hard he became _____.
16. 1882: He became a _____. (profession)
17. He was _____ and fair. (character trait)
19. France, England, and Russia were _____. (war team)
21. Countries of _____ clashed in war. (continent)
22. Second baby, _____, born.
24. Third baby, _____, born.
25. 1910: Wilson was _____ of NJ. (chief)
28. 1913: Was inaugurated twenty-_____ pres.

Presidential Puzzlers Copyright © 2005 Good Year Books

82

Woodrow Wilson
1913–1921

CROSSING OVER

DIRECTIONS

Use a pencil for this game. Using the words that are not in parentheses, find words from the following list that have the correct number of spaces and letters to fit into the crossing-over boxes. Each word has a place where it belongs. The first word is done for you. To continue, find an eight-letter word having an "n" in the seventh space. All the words tell about Woodrow Wilson.

3 letters

(practiced speeches of famous) **men**

(studied) **law** (at University of VA)

(United States sold) **war** (materials to Allies)

(balloons were used to) **spy** (on enemies)

4 letters

(1885: first) **book** (published)

(as government, passed laws to) **help** (people)

(as pres. he was honest and) **fair**

(1914: wife Ellen) **died**

(many) **rats** (in war trenches)

(1915: airplanes had) **guns** (and bombs)

(1915: Edith, second wife, helped Wilson with his) **work**

(1915: U.S. prepared an) **army**

5 letters

(moved family to CT to) **teach**

three (European Allies: France, Russia, England)

(United States sold) **wheat** (to Allies)

(U.S. banks loaned) **money** (to Allies)

(1915: pilots held) **bombs** (in their hands to throw at enemy)

(1915: United States built) **ships**

6 letters

(horrible) **deaths** (in war)

(1915: U.S.) **tanker** (sunk by Germans)

(Wilson wanted to be part of) **public** (life)

second (book published)

(1890: taught at Princeton, New) **Jersey**

(a European ally) **France**

(a European ally) **Russia**

(U.S. did not want to enter war with) **Allies**

(1915:) **Italy** (entered the war)

7 letters

(a European ally:) **England**

(U.S.) **neutral** (to stay out of European war)

(War: France fought) **Germany**

(1915) **America** (prepared for war)

(1915: Wilson) **married** (Edith Galt)

8 letters

(as a boy, Wilson wanted to be a) **minister**

(Germany sank U.S.) **merchant** (ships)

9 letters

(1902: was pres. of) **Princeton** (University)

(1913: inaugurated as 28th) **president**

(FTC: fair) **practices** (in trade and business)

airplanes (used to spy on enemy)

Woodrow Wilson
1913–1921

WORLD WAR I PAIRS
DIRECTIONS
All of the war names in the large box are written twice, except for one. Write the name of each pair on a line. (Cross off the pairs as you find them.) Then find the name of the war word that appears only once, and write it in the box.

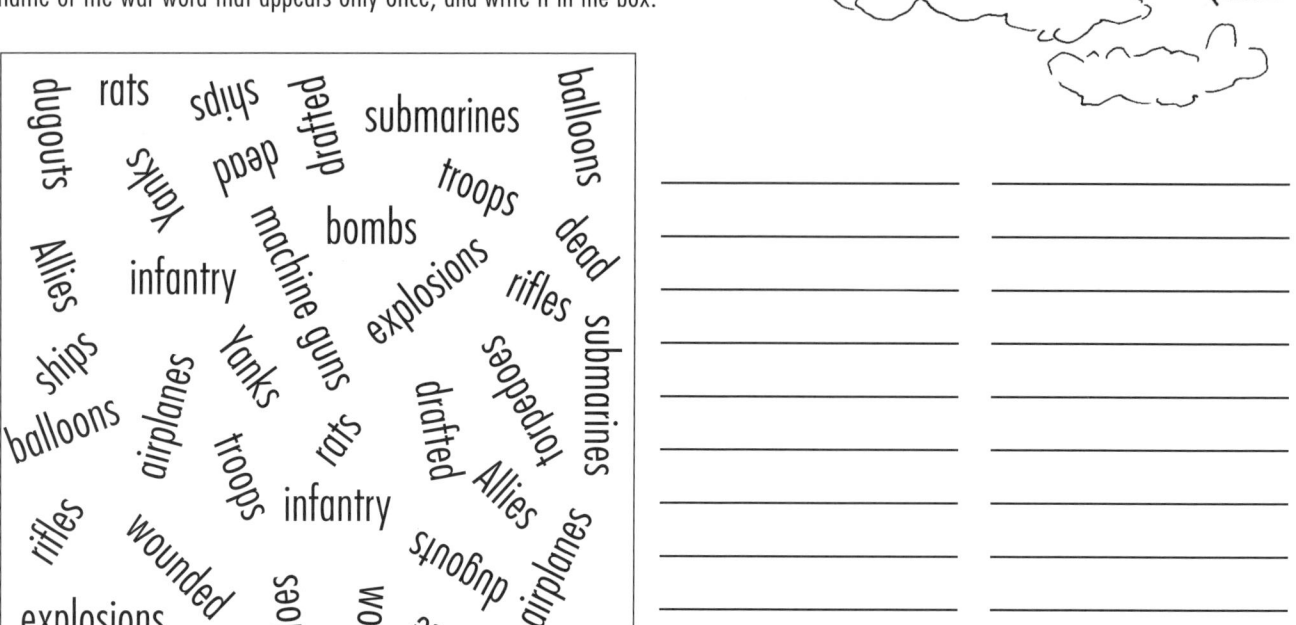

NAME THE GOVERNOR'S HOME
DIRECTIONS
Fill in the dotted lines with your answers. If they are correct, the circled letters will spell the name and location of Woodrow Wilson's home as governor.

1. Germany _____ four U.S. merchant ships.
2. U.S. men were _____ for war.
3. United States declared _____ on Germany.
4. Meat, _____, and home heating were rationed to help the war effort. (sweet)
5. Factories made _____ for soldiers. (clothing)
6. Farmers produced more _____ for food. (field products)
7. Women worked in _____.
8. By 1918, 116,000 U.S. men had died in the war and many more were _____.
9. U.S. Gen. _____ Pershing was a decorated hero.

Warren G. Harding
1921–1923

CROSSWORD PUZZLE

ACROSS

2. Went to _____ in Caledonia, OH. (place to learn)
4. As a teen he went to farms to paint the _____ red. (buildings)
7. He grew tall and _____. (mighty)
9. Birth state: _____
10. Father, George, had been a Civil War _____ for the Army. (musician)
13. Warren: oldest of _____ children
14. Liked _____ for newspapers. (used his pen)
15. Mother, Phoebe, delivered _____. (newborns)
19. He found Indian _____ on the way to school. (remains from past)
23. _____ of school newspaper (reviser)
24. Mother taught him _____. (rhymes)
25. Got a used _____ and played in the band. (horn)
29. He liked to bring out the _____ in people. (not the bad)
30. He split wood for _____ fences.
31. 1883: _____ for a newspaper. (for pay)
32. At 19, he bought the Marion _____ newspaper. (object in night sky)

DOWN

1. Father was a _____. (medical profession)
3. Born seven months after _____ War ended.
4. The Marion Star newspaper was a _____ success. (large)
5. Father's name: _____
6. Boyhood chore: chopping _____
8. In school he was good at _____. (writing words)
11. 1882: Father moved the family to _____, OH.
12. Mother's name: _____
16. Mother taught him the _____ using a burned stick on a box. (letters)
17. Boys and girls _____ him.
18. He enjoyed publishing a _____.
20. Helped father plant _____. (crop)
21. 1891: Warren and Florence were _____. (wed)
22. He liked _____ball.
26. Florence helped in the newspaper _____. (business areas)
27. 1882: He _____ school. (instructed)
28. He milked _____.

85

Warren G. Harding
1921–1923

WORD SEARCHING

DIRECTIONS

In the grid, find these words about Warren G. Harding (the words that are not in parentheses). They can go up, down, across, at an angle, forward, or backward.

(Warren wanted reporters to be) **honest**(, accurate, fair and decent)

(was one of the first persons in Marion, OH, to own an) **automobile**

(began public) **speaking**

(1898: Won a seat in the) **Ohio** (Senate)

(1903: was Lt.) **Governor** (of OH)

(1914: Was elected to U.S.) **Senate**

(had a pleasing voice and good) **manners**

(liked helping the working) **man**

(was against drinking) **alcohol**

(1916: gave keynote) **speech** (at Republican Convention in Chicago)

(1917: U.S. declared) **war** (on Germany)

(1920: he began campaigning for) **presidency**

(women, for the first time, got to) **vote**

(Harding never talked against his) **opponent** (for pres.)

(for the first time,) **radio** (broadcasted the presidential election and his father listened)

(Warren: was twenty-) **ninth** (pres.)

A	L	C	O	H	O	L	B	D	J	M	A	N
F	I	H	E	N	P	Q	S	M	T	A	G	C
Y	A	Y	C	Z	G	D	V	W	L	N	O	K
O	H	C	R	V	J	F	O	I	B	N	E	U
P	L	N	P	M	Q	V	T	W	S	E	K	S
P	O	E	R	H	O	N	E	S	T	R	Y	P
O	N	D	U	T	Z	C	F	N	B	S	D	E
N	A	I	A	H	K	M	I	J	O	N	G	E
E	E	S	R	U	T	N	S	P	I	W	Y	C
N	S	E	U	F	T	C	H	G	D	S	B	H
T	E	R	E	H	C	O	K	M	O	P	J	L
P	N	P	I	N	R	H	M	T	S	E	V	G
W	A	C	R	A	D	I	O	O	B	A	T	E
F	T	I	K	M	P	O	E	U	B	K	W	O
G	E	Y	O	R	H	W	S	J	A	I	Y	R
L	A	D	G	N	B	A	E	D	U	N	L	G
V	C	F	R	O	N	R	E	V	O	G	H	E

86

Warren G. Harding
1921–1923

NUMBER CODE

DIRECTIONS

Look at the numbers under each line. Find the matching numbers in the code box, and write the letters on the corresponding answer lines.

A - 1	N - 14
B - 2	O - 15
C - 3	P - 16
D - 4	Q - 17
E - 5	R - 18
F - 6	S - 19
G - 7	T - 20
H - 8	U - 21
I - 9	V - 22
J - 10	W - 23
K - 11	X - 24
L - 12	Y - 25
M - 13	Z - 26

1. For the first time, president and vice-president rode to the inauguration in a __ __ __ .
   3 1 18

2. There was neither a parade nor inaugural __ __ __ __ , so the gov't was saved
   2 1 12 12

   the __ __ __ __ __ __ __ .
   5 24 16 5 14 19 5

3. Harding had goals: peace treaty with __ __ __ __ __ __ __ , lower government expenses,
   7 5 18 13 1 14 25

   and workers switching to peacetime production of materials.

4. Each Allied country took one unidentified soldier's __ __ __ __ and buried it in an honored __ __ __ __ to represent
   2 15 4 25   20 15 13 2

   all soldiers who had died.

5. __ __ __ __ __ __ __ __ __ Cemetery, in the Washington, D.C., area, is the resting place
   1 18 12 9 14 7 20 15 14

   for many soldiers killed in U.S. wars.

6. Harding __ __ __ __ __ __ __ __ to people's concerns and tried to make __ __ __ __ __ __ __ .
           12 9 19 20 5 14 5 4   3 8 1 14 7 5 19

7. Harding's term had a __ __ __ __ __ __ __ __ __ __ __ __ __ .
                          2 1 12 1 14 3 5 4 2 21 4 7 5 20

8. He helped __ __ __ __ __ __ __ and coal __ __ __ __ __ __ .
              6 1 18 13 5 18 19   13 9 14 5 18 19

9. Steel companies cut twelve-hour __ __ __ __ days to eight hours.
                                    23 15 18 11

10. Harding tried to get benefits for wounded __ __ __ __ __ __ __ __ and sailors.
                                                19 15 12 4 9 5 18 19

11. Florence welcomed many visitors to the __ __ __ __ __ House.
                                            23 8 9 20 5

12. On a U.S. tour, making many speeches, Harding __ __ __ __ .
                                                    4 9 5 4

87

Calvin Coolidge
1923–1929

CROSSWORD PUZZLE

ACROSS

1. 1904: He met Grace, teacher of _____. (hearing impaired)
4. Won a $150 _____ for writing.
7. Birth state: _____
9. _____ Coolidge gave him forty acres of land. (forefather)
11. At three, he fell from a horse; _____ his arm.
14. Father's name: _____
15. 1875: Sister _____ was born.
17. Boyhood chore: taking cattle to _____.
22. He wrote very _____.
23. 1909: Was elected _____ of Northampton, MA. (highest official)
26. 1897: He became a _____. (profession)
28. 1906: Son John was _____.
29. Was sent to the State _____ for two terms.
30. 1911: Was elected to MA _____; became Senate pres.

DOWN

2. Boyhood chore: splitting _____ wood
3. Father owned a _____ store. (variety)
5. Father owned farm _____. (cattle, sheep, horses)
6. 1905: Calvin and Grace were _____.
7. Mother's name: _____
8. As a child, had _____ hair and freckles.
10. Worked hard; was very _____. (character trait)
12. Boyhood farm: Sheared _____ and brought in crops.
13. As a boy: liked April with maple _____-making
14. Born: _____ 4, 1872
16. Boyhood: Dug potatoes; picked _____ from trees. (fruit)
18. 1900: _____ city attorney in MA. (chosen)
19. 1907: Worked to get voting rights for _____.
20. 1907: Worked to get safer _____ conditions for women and children.
21. 1916: He was elected _____ governor of MA. (second in command)
24. 1908: Second son, _____, was born.
25. 1906: Was elected to _____ of Representatives.
27. He was determined to be useful in the _____. (planet)

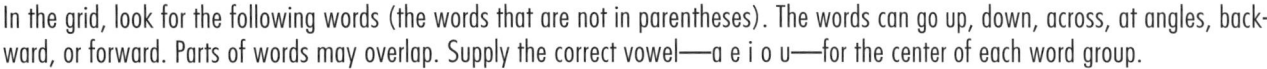

Calvin Coolidge
1923–1929

SUPPLY THE VOWEL
DIRECTIONS
In the grid, look for the following words (the words that are not in parentheses). The words can go up, down, across, at angles, backward, or forward. Parts of words may overlap. Supply the correct vowel—a e i o u—for the center of each word group.

(when Calvin was 12, his mother) **died**
(Calvin's wife) **Grace**
(1919: he became) **governor** (of MA)
(Calvin married Grace, a teacher of the) **deaf**
(1920s: raccoon) **coats** (were popular)
(people could) **buy** (phonographs)
(sister) **Abigail** (died at 13)
(people could buy) **telephones**
(baseball player Babe) **Ruth** (was famous)

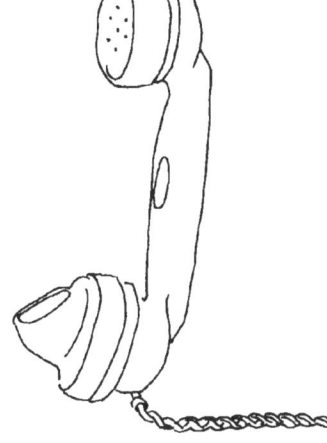

B	G	F	S	J	A	E	C	G	I	D	H	F
L	E	M	E	P	R	K	O	N	R	S	R	U
V	A	C	N	O	Y	N	I	V	L	○	C	T
C	D	E	○	D	R	W	F	J	N	B	C	B
G	I	D	H	V	O	H	M	C	L	I	K	E
V	A	N	C	O	N	T	E	U	S	G	P	R
R	A	W	A	C	R	B	E	S	D	A	Z	Y
H	G	S	M	D	E	J	T	I	E	I	F	K
M	L	E	N	P	V	A	P	Q	T	L	R	O
T	C	N	S	J	○	H	N	B	A	W	Y	L
D	V	O	G	C	G	L	A	F	R	H	N	K
U	E	H	P	F	O	I	E	A	U	Z	E	B
R	H	P	A	T	Y	J	S	B	G	S	C	M
A	M	○	R	I	C	A	G	R	○	T	H	E
U	D	L	A	L	W	F	M	O	A	Y	D	P
H	V	E	I	R	K	T	H	C	N	A	N	S
O	J	T	V	W	T	B	E	U	I	D	R	Y

(1919: Calvin welcomed soldiers home from) **France**
(1920: Harding Pres.; Coolidge) **vice**(-pres.)
(second son) **Calvin**, (Jr. died of blood poisoning)
(1925: Coolidge was) **inaugurated** (pres.)
(people could buy washing) **machines**
(1925: Calvin's inaugural speech was heard on) **radio**
(1926: Adm. Byrd and Floyd Bennett flew over the North) **Pole**
(son) **John**
(Pres. Harding died of a) **heart** (attack; Coolidge became pres.)
(Calvin's presidency saw great prosperity in) **America**
(Calvin liked to study each room in the White) **House**

89

Calvin Coolidge
1923–1929

SCRAMBLED WORDS
DIRECTIONS
Unscramble the words and write the answers on the lines provided. (Use scrap paper to work out your answers.)

1. Chief Justice ATTF administered Coolidge's inaugural AHOT. _____ _____

2. Meaning of *Prohibition:* the sale of alcoholic KSIDRN was unlawful in the United States. _____

3. 1927: Charles Lindbergh made the first solo flight across the ANTTICAL Ocean. _____

4. The Coolidge family had TSPE in the White House. _____

5. Coolidge lowered SAETX and brought down the U.S. TBDE. _____ _____

6. J. Edgar EOORHV was director of the FBI. _____

7. 1927: Coolidge announced that he would not run for NEITRDPSE again. _____

8. 1933: Calvin died of a TREHA attack. _____

9. Calvin was EIUBRD at Plymouth Notch, VT. _____

NUMBER CODE
DIRECTIONS
Look at the numbers under each line. Find the matching numbers in the code box, and write the letters on the corresponding answer lines.

A - 1	N - 14
B - 2	O - 15
C - 3	P - 16
D - 4	Q - 17
E - 5	R - 18
F - 6	S - 19
G - 7	T - 20
H - 8	U - 21
I - 9	V - 22
J - 10	W - 23
K - 11	X - 24
L - 12	Y - 25
M - 13	Z - 26

1. Calvin __ __ __ __ __ __ __ __ __ __ __ and brought the
   12 15 23 5 18 5 4 20 1 24 5 19

   __ __ __ __ __ __ __ __ __ __ .
   21 19 4 5 2 20 4 15 23 14

2. Calvin __ __ __ __ __ __ __ __ __ __ __ __ __ __ __ __ __
   4 9 4 14 15 20 23 1 14 20 20 15 18 21 14 6 15 18

   __ .
   16 18 5 19 9 4 5 14 20 20 8 5 19 5 3 15 14 4 20 9 13 5

3. He __ __ __ __ __ __ __ __ __ __ __ . One afternoon at the White House, Calvin __ __ __ __ __
   12 9 11 5 4 20 15 10 15 11 5   20 15 15 11 1

   __
   14 1 16 23 8 5 14 1 19 5 18 22 1 14 20 1 23 1 11 5 14 5 4

   __ __ __ , Calvin asked, " __
   8 9 13   9 19 20 8 5 3 15 21 14 20 18 25 19 20 9 12 12

   __ __ __ __ ?"
   8 5 18 5

4. Calvin was a __ __ __ __ __ __ __ __ __ __ __ __ __ , but he __ __ __ __ __ __ __ __ __
   22 5 18 25 17 21 9 5 20 13 1 14   12 9 19 20 5 14 5 4

   well to __ __ __ __ __ __ __ __ __ that was __ __ __ __ __ __ __
   5 22 5 18 25 20 8 9 14 7   19 16 15 11 5 14

Herbert C. Hoover
1929–1933

DOWN

1. The Hoovers were plain people called _____. (a church denomination)
2. Herbert and Lou lived in Tientsin, _____. (Asia)
3. Australia: A camel _____ his leg. (teeth)
4. The Boxers, rebels, in China used _____ fire to kill Westerners. (weapon)
6. Birthplace: West Branch, _____.
7. After parents died, Herbert, Theodore, and May became _____. (without parents)
8. Boyhood chore: hoeing and pulling up _____ (unwanted plants)
9. Uncle Henry, a doctor, took Herbert along to visit his _____. (sick)
12. Herbert had one brother, Theodore, and one sister _____.
13. A silver mine made his company and him _____. (rich)
16. Tientsin: Westerners stacked _____ of food as protection from shelling. (sacks)
18. Stanford University: He met Lou in _____ class. (study of rocks, earth)
19. He was _____. (shy)
21. Father's name: _____

CROSSWORD PUZZLE
ACROSS

2. Australian desert had very little water so he rode a _____ to work, not a horse. (animal)
3. Father's occupation: _____ (owned a forge)
4. Herbert managed a _____ mine in Australia. (valuable metal)
5. 1885: At 11, Herbert went by _____ to Oregon, to live with Uncle Henry.
8. Quakers managed money _____. (intelligently)
10. Mother died of _____. (lung illness)
11. Father died of _____ problems. (in chest)
12. 1899: Herbert and Lou were _____. (wed)
14. Herbert _____ to be an engineer. (learned)
15. He inspected _____ for Bewick, Moreing Co. (underground excavations)
17. Born: _____ 10, 1874
19. Childhood: Hunted potato _____; got 1¢ for every 100 insects.
20. Mother's name: _____
22. He wanted the Chinese to _____ in the control of mines. (divide)
23. Boyhood chore: splitting _____

Presidential Puzzlers Copyright © 2005 Good Year Books

Herbert C. Hoover
1929–1933

CROSSING OVER

DIRECTIONS
Use a pencil for this game. Find words from the following list that have the correct number of spaces and letters to fit into the crossing-over boxes (the words not in parentheses). Each word has a place where it belongs. The first word is done for you. To continue, find an eight-letter word having an "a" in the fourth space. All the words tell about Herbert Hoover.

3 letters
(Herbert urged) **men** (to invest in good mines)
(1917: U.S. entered European) **war**
(1903:) **son** (Herbert born)

4 letters
army (troops rescued Westerners in Tientsin)
(after China rebellion, Herbert managed) **coal** (mines)
(Burma: Silver in the mine made Herbert and owners) **rich**
(1917: Herbert was) **food** (administrator for the war)
(In World War I, U.S. women were asked to cook) **fish** (not red meat)

5 letters
(father's name) **Jesse**
(mother's name) **Hulda**
(parents died; he lived with his Uncle) **Henry**
(1901: Belgium took control of Chinese coal) **mines**
(he left) **China** (due to Belgium's greed)
(1907: baby) **Allan** (born)
(earned more) **money** (in his own business)
(WW I: farmers urged to raise more) **crops**
(in Burma: Hoover saw) **tiger** (tracks in mine; left quickly)
(Europe gave) **honor** (to Herbert for his work)

6 letters
(Herbert's uncle was a) **doctor**
(WW I: managed food supplies for army and) **allies**
(WW I: asked Americans to be) **saving**
(WW I: extra grain) **stored**
(Herbert went to) **Europe** (to organize food after WW I)

7 letters
(son) **Herbert** (born)
(Tientsin: Lou helped care for the) **wounded**
(1901: Belgium didn't want) **Chinese** (to share control of (mines)
(he liked) **America** (best)

8 letters
(WW I: he tried to feed and clothe) **starving** (children)
(1905:) **traveled** (worldwide checking mines)

(he was called the "Great) **Engineer**"
(WW I: U.S. women were asked to cook more) **potatoes**
(WW I: he handled food supplies and) **shipping**

9 letters
(took baby Herbert to) **Australia** (in a basket)
(saw many poor people in other) **countries**
(against big, rich) **companies** (that underpaid workers)

Herbert C. Hoover
1929–1933

SKYSCRAPER
DIRECTIONS
Write your answers in the boxes. The circled letters will help you.

1. Abbr. for Iowa (home state)
2. 1927: _____ was invented. (abbr. for something we watch)
3. A huge _____ was built in the west to produce electric power.
4. 1928: America's economy was very _____.
5. 1929: _____ was inaugurated president.
6. 1929: The stock _____ crashed.
7. 1929: Men lost their _____.
8. 1929: People lost their _____ and couldn't buy things.
9. 1929: _____ made no products. (industrial buildings)
10. 1929: Banks had no money, so they _____.
11. Hoover spent many long hours trying to end the Great _____, but he couldn't.

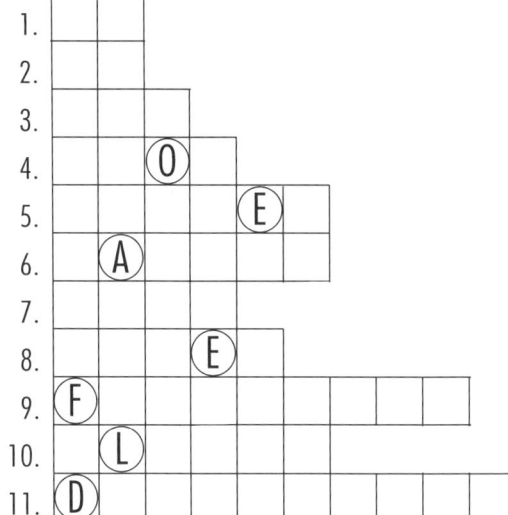

CLUE
DIRECTIONS
Each set of lines has vowels and an occasional consonant to help you determine the correct answer. All the words tell about Herbert Hoover.

1. 1933: Franklin __ o o __ e __ e __ __ was inaugurated president.
2. 1933: Roosevelt permitted the name of Hoover Dam to be changed to B o u __ __ e __ Dam.
3. Hoover warned against Roosevelt spending too much gov't __ o __ e __.
4. 1941: Japan __ o m __ e __ __ e a __ __ __ a __ __ o __.
5. 1941: W o __ __ __ __ a __ II began.
6. 1943: The Allies bombed __ e __ m a __ __.
7. 1944: Wife Lou __ i e __ of a __ e a __ __ attack.
8. 1945: Pres. Roosevelt died; Vice-Pres. __ r u __ a __ became pres.
9. 1945: Pres. Truman invited Hoover to the __ __ i __ e __ o u __ e.
10. 1946: Hoover again organized __ o o __ s u __ __ __ i e __ for Europe.
11. 1947: Hoover saved the U.S. gov't. __ i __ __ i o __ __ of dollars.
12. 1947: Boulder Dam was renamed __ o o __ e __ Dam.
13. 1952: Dwight D. E i __ e __ __ o __ e __ became president.
14. 1964: Herbert Hoover __ i e __.

93

Franklin D. Roosevelt
1933–1945

CROSSWORD PUZZLE

ACROSS

2. Father's name: _____
4. Mother's name: _____
7. Sara was James's _____ wife.
8. Roosevelts' estate home: _____ Park
9. James was vice-_____ of a railway.
11. Franklin's favorite pet was a _____
13. He started dating _____ Roosevelt, a distant cousin.
17. Liked to explore the _____ at Hyde Park.
18. Was taught by _____ until he was 14.
19. Boyhood disease: scarlet _____
20. He liked to _____ with his father. (go places)
22. Was heartbroken when father _____.
24. Father and he sailed _____. (with each other)
26. Franklin was president of Harvard's _____. (periodical)
27. Eleanor: favorite _____ of Teddy Roosevelt (He was her uncle.)

DOWN

1. Until he was five, he wore _____. (clothing)
2. Born: _____ 30, 1882
3. He liked to _____ in the Hudson R.
4. Many _____ at both homes waited on them. (employees)
5. James was very _____. (wealthy)
6. He had a large estate home on the _____ R.
10. The estate house was called _____.
12. Had a bow and _____ to shoot.
14. Was not good at _____. (athletics)
15. Eleanor was _____ for the poor. (wanting to help)
16. Franklin and Eleanor: _____ living children
18. As a boy, Franklin built a _____ house near the Hudson R.
21. As a boy, he and his _____ spent much time together.
23. Was excellent at _____. (arguing issues)
25. Eleanor liked to _____ Uncle Teddy at the White House. (spend time)

Franklin D. Roosevelt
1933–1945

WORD SEARCHING

DIRECTIONS
In the grid, find these words about Franklin D. Roosevelt (the words that are not in parentheses). They can go up, down, across, at an angle, forward, or backward.

E	C	I	F	C	O	U	N	T	R	I	E	S
L	R	D	J	S	C	T	B	N	J	J	A	T
Q	A	R	P	O	O	R	H	G	H	A	K	J
V	S	U	P	A	P	B	C	B	M	G	P	A	I
D	H	H	W	O	V	S	F	B	D	A	H	G
F	E	K	A	Y	U	E	F	R	A	N	C	E
Y	D	W	O	R	S	C	J	E	W	S	N	L
L	R	M	I	K	B	J	M	L	E	R	P	O
P	T	T	N	I	S	O	W	T	U	W	A	R
L	R	N	V	T	Y	J	R	I	F	T	K	G
O	U	E	C	A	D	H	R	H	L	E	Y	M
N	S	D	I	L	N	S	C	P	O	D	N	A
D	S	I	A	Y	N	I	V	W	C	U	A	N
O	I	S	T	G	E	O	M	P	A	V	M	T
N	A	E	F	R	C	E	B	R	X	W	R	E
G	B	R	K	M	I	L	S	H	I	A	E	I
J	A	P	R	O	J	E	C	T	S	T	G	V

(1929: stock market) **crashed**

(1929: banks closed, businesses failed, men lost) **jobs**

(1929: as governor, he provided jobs for the) **poor**

(1933: Franklin was inaugurated) **president** (and promised people work)

(1933: many public works) **projects** (gave people jobs)

(1939: England and France declared war on) **Germany**

(Germany, Italy, and Japan, were called) **Axis** (Powers)

(Germany: Hitler built an empire called Third) **Reich**

Hitler (was dictator and got rid of anyone opposing him)

(Hitler took over eight) **countries**

(Hitler had more than 6,000,000) **Jews** (killed)

(1940: Axis Powers conquered) **France**

(1940: Japan conquered) **Vietnam**

(1941: Japan bombed Pearl) **Harbor** (in Hawaii)

(1941: Germany attacked) **Russia**

(1941: U.S. declared war on) **Japan**

(1941: Germany and) **Italy** (declared war on the U.S.)

(1942: Germany bombed) **London**

(1942: U.S. promised England) **war** (supplies)

95

Franklin D. Roosevelt
1933–1945

NAME THE ROOSEVELTS' SUMMER HOME AND LOCATION

DIRECTIONS

Fill in the dotted lines with your answers. If they are correct, the circled letters will spell the name and location of the Roosevelts' summer home.

1. Pres. Theodore Roosevelt was Franklin's _____. (relative)
2. Franklin went to school at _____ University.
3. 1905: Franklin and Eleanor were _____.
4. Franklin and Eleanor went to _____ on their wedding trip. (continent)
5. At 25, Franklin was elected to the New _____ Senate.
6. 1906: Baby Anna was _____.
7. Eleanor was very _____. (bright)
8. 1905: Franklin went to _____ school. (legal)
9. As Senator he worked to _____ working men and farmers; supported women's rights.
10. Franklin campaigned for _____ for president.
11. Franklin was appointed by Wilson as _____ sec'y of the navy. (second in command)
12. Franklin kept the Navy efficient, _____, and well-planned. (mighty)
13. 1917: The United States entered World War II; Franklin went to Europe to _____ Navy facilities. (look over)
14. Franklin was president of the Boy Scouts of _____.
15. 1921: _____, 39, became ill with polio.
16. With _____ on his legs, Franklin became governor of New York. (supports)
17. 1929: The stock market _____. (fell)
18. Depression (1929): _____ closed; men were out of work; people were hungry.

96

Harry S. Truman
1945–1953

CROSSWORD PUZZLE

ACROSS

5. He was _____ and good in school. (bright)
6. Born: _____ 8, 1884
7. Birth state: _____
11. At 8, he needed _____ to see well.
12. Read about _____ people. (well-known)
14. 1886: brother, Vivian, was _____. (birth)
17. At 14, he had read the _____ three times. (Scriptures)
19. 1905: Signed up with the _____ Guard.
20. Poor _____ kept him out of West Point. (seeing)
22. First job: Earned $3 per week for opening a _____ at 6:30 A.M.
26. 1924: Trumans' baby, _____, was born.
28. 1919: Harry and Bess were _____.
29. 1902: He worked in a _____. (where money is kept)
30. 1922: Was elected _____. (gave verdicts)

DOWN

1. At 14, he had read all the books in the public _____.
2. At 5, Harry could _____. (recite words)
3. _____ Wallace was a childhood friend.
4. 1906–1916: Made family farm _____. (prosperous)
6. Mother's name: _____
8. Father moved his family to _____, MO.
9. 1890: _____, Mary Jane, was born. (sibling)
10. Wife Bess had _____ hair and blue eyes.
13. School: Skipped from second to _____ grade.
15. 1917: Lt. Truman fought in _____. (country)
16. Liked books about _____. (times past)
18. Neighbor children came to his farm to _____.
21. 1926: As a judge, he _____ county roads. (made better)
23. 1917: Became Capt. Harry _____.
24. In gov't, he made sure the money _____ got full value.
25. His men's wear store _____. (unsuccessful)
27. It took him 15 years to pay the _____ for the failed store.

Harry S. Truman
1945–1953

SUPPLY THE VOWEL

DIRECTIONS

In the grid, look for the following words (the words that are not in parentheses). The words can go up, down, across, at angles, backward, or forward. Parts of words may overlap. Supply the correct vowel—a e i o u—for the center of each word group.

- (father's name) **John**
- (other children made) **fun** (of his glasses)
- (1934: elected to U.S.) **Senate**
- (worked hard for reelection of) **Roosevelt**
- (always kept his campaign) **promises**
- (1941) **urged** (Congress to investigate defense spending)
- (1941) **chairman** (of defense-spending committee)
- (was always) **honest**
- (1944: campaigned for) **ailing** (Roosevelt)
- (1944: elected) **vice** (-pres.)
- (1945: Truman and Roosevelt took oaths at the White) **House**
- (1945: Roosevelt) **died**
- (1945:) **Truman** (inaugurated president)
- (1945: Truman a) **strong** (pres. who took charge)
- (1945: helped the United) **Nations** (become a reality)
- (1945: Russia was a threat to Europe's) **peace**
- (1945: Russia) **broke** (promises)
- (1945: Japan ignored warnings) **atomic** (bomb was dropped)
- (1945:) **Japan** (surrendered)
- (1945: Truman warned Congress about) **recession** (after war)

B	F	H	D	L	N	K	A	J	C	T	N	H
E	M	I	G	A	W	U	T	O	F	R	O	Y
P	N	S	P	R	C	D	E	G	R	O	C	A
C	H	O	I	R	M	A	N	I	S	M	N	H
D	J	I	T	K	E	B	J	E	E	A	F	G
L	N	L	P	I	V	T	O	T	S	N	R	M
U	Y	I	T	W	O	E	A	H	J	B	F	A
D	K	N	I	S	P	N	S	G	P	R	M	C
L	O	G	D	I	O	D	S	T	Y	T	W	B
N	A	S	U	S	A	N	G	F	D	L	H	C
V	I	E	O	E	C	S	O	J	N	E	W	Y
J	C	S	V	P	E	R	U	H	T	V	B	E
N	O	O	S	S	E	C	E	R	F	E	D	E
K	C	M	M	A	I	L	G	C	J	S	K	C
E	L	O	P	O	R	O	S	T	R	O	N	G
M	B	R	J	S	T	W	U	A	R	O	H	N
K	V	P	A	H	Y	A	T	B	M	R	D	N

98

Harry S. Truman
1945–1953

SAME FIRST LETTER
DIRECTIONS
Find two words that begin with the same letter for each of these letters. The circled letter is the first letter for each answer.

Example:

S
S **T R I K E**
Coal miners threatened to ____.
S **H I P S**
North Korea invaded South Korea; Truman sent ____ and planes to attack.

C
C _ _ _ _ _ _ _ He took ____ of the coal mines.
C _ _ _ _ _ _ _ He fired two ____ members who caused trouble.

R
R _ _ _ _ _ _ _ _ _ took over European countries.
R _ _ _ _ Russia blockaded the main ____ going into Berlin.

A
A _ _ _ _ Truman told striking railroad workers he'd draft them into the ____.
A _ _ He sent foreign ____ to protect Greece and Turkey from Russia.

P
P _ _ _ _ _ Truman sent supplies to Berlin by ____.
P _ _ _ _ _ _ _ _ _ Truman and Dewey ran for ____.

R
R _ _ _ _ _ _ _ _ Truman was ____ president.
R _ _ _ _ _ _ _ _ Julius and Ethel ____ were executed for giving secret information to Russia.

C
C _ _ _ _ _ _ _ _ _ U.S. aid was given to European ____.
C _ _ _ _ _ _ _ _ _ Suspected ____ in the U.S. were jailed.

NUMBER CODE
DIRECTIONS
Look at the numbers under each line. Find the matching numbers in the code box, and write the letters on the corresponding answer lines.

1. In 1952, Truman did _ _ _ _ _ _ _ _
   $\overline{14}\ \overline{15}\ \overline{20}\ \overline{}\ \overline{18}\ \overline{21}\ \overline{14}\ \overline{}\ \overline{6}\ \overline{15}\ \overline{18}$
   _ _ _ _ _ _ _ _ _ again.
   $\overline{16}\ \overline{18}\ \overline{5}\ \overline{19}\ \overline{9}\ \overline{4}\ \overline{5}\ \overline{14}\ \overline{20}$

2. In 1953, the Trumans $\overline{18}\ \overline{5}\ \overline{20}\ \overline{21}\ \overline{18}\ \overline{14}\ \overline{5}\ \overline{4}$ to Independence, Missouri.

3. In 1953, people $\overline{3}\ \overline{8}\ \overline{5}\ \overline{5}\ \overline{18}\ \overline{5}\ \overline{4}$ the Trumans from
   $\overline{11}\ \overline{1}\ \overline{14}\ \overline{19}\ \overline{1}\ \overline{19}\ \overline{}\ \overline{3}\ \overline{9}\ \overline{20}\ \overline{25}$ to Independence, Missouri.

4. Truman $\overline{23}\ \overline{18}\ \overline{15}\ \overline{20}\ \overline{5}$ two $\overline{2}\ \overline{15}\ \overline{15}\ \overline{11}\ \overline{19}$.

5. He $\overline{23}\ \overline{1}\ \overline{12}\ \overline{11}\ \overline{5}\ \overline{4}\ \overline{}\ \overline{2}\ \overline{18}\ \overline{9}\ \overline{19}\ \overline{11}\ \overline{25}$ nearly every day until he was 88.

6. In 1972, Truman $\overline{4}\ \overline{9}\ \overline{5}\ \overline{4}$.

7. In 1972, he was $\overline{2}\ \overline{21}\ \overline{18}\ \overline{9}\ \overline{5}\ \overline{4}$ in Independence, Missouri.

A - 1	N - 14
B - 2	O - 15
C - 3	P - 16
D - 4	Q - 17
E - 5	R - 18
F - 6	S - 19
G - 7	T - 20
H - 8	U - 21
I - 9	V - 22
J - 10	W - 23
K - 11	X - 24
L - 12	Y - 25
M - 13	Z - 26

Dwight D. Eisenhower
1953–1961

CROSSWORD PUZZLE

ACROSS

1. Dwight (Ike) met Mamie and fell in _____.
5. 1916: He gave Mamie his class ring as a _____ promise. (wedding)
6. The six Eisenhower boys helped Mother with laundry, _____, and cooking. (dinnerware)
8. Mother's name: _____
10. 1916: In spare time he coached football in San _____, TX.
13. Had _____ living brothers.
16. 1918: Ike trained soldiers in _____ warfare. (heavy vehicle)
17. Ike and brothers read from the _____. (holy book)
18. Ike and brothers grew _____ to sell. (produce)
20. 1915: He met a pretty young woman, _____, in Texas.
21. Father moved the family to a bigger _____. (dwelling)
22. David and Ida had _____ sons; one died.
24. _____ and trucks were used in WW I.
27. 1915: Ike graduated from West _____.
28. West Point: a _____ Academy in NY
29. 1918: Ike was promoted to _____. (rank)
31. 1917: Germany _____ U.S. ships. (used underwater missile)

DOWN

1. 1915: Ike was sent to Ft. Sam Houston as a Second _____. (rank)
2. Father's name: _____
3. Ike liked to read about _____. (battles)
4. Birthplace: Denison, _____
7. 1917: Airplanes were used in war for the first _____.
9. 1891: Father moved the family to _____, TX.
11. Ike's parents were _____. (took God seriously)
12. In school, he liked _____ best. (subject)
14. Ft. Leavenworth: Graduated _____ in class of 275. (rank)
15. Outlaw Pancho Villa harrassed _____ along U.S. border. (frontiers)
19. With vegetable money, Ike and brothers bought _____ mitts.
23. 1917: Pres. Wilson declared war on _____.
25. High school: Ike liked all kinds of _____. (athletics)
26. Born: _____, 1890
30. West Point trained young _____ to be army officers.

Dwight D. Eisenhower
1953–1961

CROSSING OVER

DIRECTIONS

Use a pencil for this game. Using the words that are not in parentheses, find words from the following list that have the correct number of spaces and letters to fit into the crossing-over boxes. Each word has a place where it belongs. The first word is done for you. To continue, find a ten-letter word with an "n" in the last space. All the words tell about Dwight D. Eisenhower.

7 Letters

(1941: promoted to Brig.) **General**

(1942: sent to) **England** (to meet with Allied leaders)

(1945: given a hero's) **welcome** (in U.S.)

8 Letters

(1940–1941: organized training, feeding, housing of many) **soldiers**

(1945:) **Russians** (captured countries in Europe)

(1943: Allies) **captured** (Sicily from Germans)

9 Letters

(1918: drove with army truck convoy from Washington, D.C., to San) **Francisco**

(worked with Gen'l Douglas) **MacArthur**

(1942: Germany had many) **victories** (in Europe)

10 Letters

(1941: summoned to) **Washington** (after Japan attacked)

11 Letters

(1945: Germany) **surrendered**

3 letters

(1941) **son** (John at West Point)

(1948: people wanted) **Ike** (for pres.)

(1929: Ike studied possibility of factories making) **war** (supplies if needed)

4 letters

(1909: graduated from) **high** (school)

(1945: promoted to Chief of Staff in U.S.) **Army**

(1951: Pres. Truman sent Ike to Europe to help organize) **NATO**

5 letters

(1896: Ike in) **first** (grade)

(1918: got) **medal** (for troop training)

(1922–1924: stationed at Panama) **Canal**

(1940: helped) **train** (U.S. soldiers)

(1941) **Chief** (of Staff, Third Army, for more than 300,000 men)

(1941: U.S. entered) **World** (War II)

(1943: Allies invaded) **Italy** (and gov't surrendered)

6 letters

(Ike's friend, Gen.) **Conner** (predicted WW II)

(1928: worked at a military base in Paris,) **France**

(1939: German dictator) **Hitler** (killed many Jews)

(Hitler at war against countries in) **Europe**

(Hitler attacked) **Poland**

(1941: Japan attacked Pearl) **Harbor**

(1941: Ike) **famous** (in U.S.)

(1942: Commander of) **Allied** (Forces in Europe)

(1942: Allies invaded N.) **Africa**

(1943: much of N. Africa) **seized** (from Germans)

101

Dwight D. Eisenhower
1953–1961

SCRAMBLED WORDS
DIRECTIONS
Unscramble the words, and write the answers on the lines provided. (Use scrap paper to work out your answers.)

1. 1952: Ike was elected EDNRTESPI; and ONNXI, vice-pres. _____ _____
2. 1952: Russian EEDLRA, Joseph Stalin, died. _____
3. 1954: HCLOSSO in the U.S. were integrated. _____
4. 1955: Ike had a TEHAR attack. _____
5. 1955: Martin Luther NIKG marched for LVICI rights. _____ _____
6. 1957: Russia sent a satellite called *KPSUINT* into space. _____
7. A nuclear RMSBIUAEN, *Seawolf,* was completed. _____
8. 1961: Ike and Mamie retired to their MAFR in Gettysburg, PA. _____
9. 1969: Ike EDID. _____
10. He was buried in ENBEALI, KS. _____

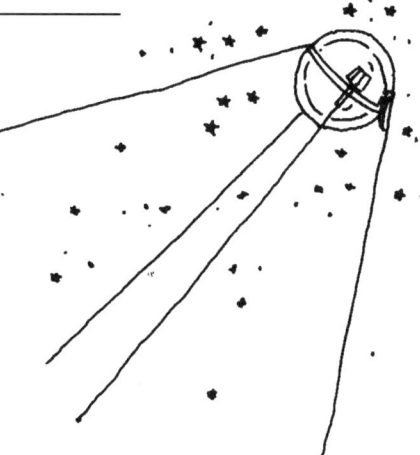

NUMBER CODE
DIRECTIONS
Look at the numbers under each line. Find the matching numbers in the code box, and write the letters on the corresponding answer lines.

1. As a boy, Ike was called __ __ __ __ __ __ __ __ __ __ __.
    4 23 9 7 8 20 4 1 22 9 4

2. His brothers were named __ __ __ __ __ __' __ __ __ __ __' __ __ __ __',
    1 18 20 8 21 18' 5 4 7 1 18' 18 18 15 25'

    __ __ __ __, and __ __ __ __ __ __ __.
    5 1 18 12   13 9 12 20 15 14

3. In school, classmates called him __ __ __ __ __ __ __ __. His older brother Edgar
    12 9 20 20 12 5 9 11 5

    was called __ __ __ __ __ __.
    2 9 7 9 11 5

4. Ike's first son, __ __ __ __ __ __ __ __ __ __, __ __ __ __ of
    4 15 21 4 4 23 9 7 8 20, 4 9 5 4

    __ __ __ __ __ __ __ __ __ __ __ at three years of age.
    19 3 1 18 12 5 20 6 5 22 5 18

5. Ike's __ __ __ __ __ __ __, __ __ __ __ __ __ __ __ __ __, was born in 1922.
    19 5 3 15 14 4   19 15 14 10 15 8 14

6. John had a son, __ __ __ __ __, who married __ __ __ __ __ '
    4 1 22 9 4   14 9 24 15 14 19

    __ __ __ __ __ __ __ __ __ __ __ __.
    4 1 21 7 8 20 5 18 10 21 12 9 5

A - 1	N - 14
B - 2	O - 15
C - 3	P - 16
D - 4	Q - 17
E - 5	R - 18
F - 6	S - 19
G - 7	T - 20
H - 8	U - 21
I - 9	V - 22
J - 10	W - 23
K - 11	X - 24
L - 12	Y - 25
M - 13	Z - 26

Presidential Puzzlers Copyright © 2005 Good Year Books.

John F. Kennedy
1961–1963

CROSSWORD PUZZLE

ACROSS
1. John, called Jack, wrote a book about England and war that became well-_____.
3. Father's name: _____
6. Recovering from _____, Jack had a tutor for schoolwork. (operation)
9. Birthplace: Brookline, _____
11. 1941: Joined the _____. (branch of service)
13. Father became a multi_____. (rich)
14. Childhood disease: whooping _____
17. Ancestry: _____
19. John's nickname: _____
22. Had an operation for _____. (abdominal inflammation)
25. 1934: Joseph was ambassador to _____.
26. Played _____ball in college, but was hurt.

DOWN
2. England and France at _____ with Germany
4. Had _____ brothers and sisters.
5. Joseph was a bank _____. (chief)
6. Loved to go out in a _____ boat.
7. World War II: in charge of a _____ gunboat— PT 109
8. Mother's name: _____
9. Childhood disease: _____ (spots)
10. Joseph was _____ with his children. (demanding)
12. Childhood disease: _____ (difficult breathing)
13. Joseph bought a _____ in NY. (huge house)
15. Jack was well-_____ by others.
16. 1939: He talked to _____ survivors of a torpedoed ship. (from U.S.)
18. Kennedys' summer home: _____ Port, MA
20. 1939: Germany sank an English ship near _____. (north of England)
21. Liked getting into _____ at school. (pranks)
23. 1939: Germany invaded _____. (country)
24. 1944: Brother Joe, Navy _____, was killed. (flyer)

103

John F. Kennedy
1961–1963

WORD SEARCHING
DIRECTIONS
In the grid, find these words about John F. Kennedy (the words that are not in parentheses). They can go up, down, across, at an angle, forward, or backward.

- (Jack) **worked** (for his ambassador father in England)
- (at 28, Jack wrote for a) **newspaper**
- (1946: he worked hard to get elected as) **congressman**
- (1947: at 30, took Congressional oath of office in) **Washington**
- (1952: ran for U.S.) **Senate**
- (1952: Jack met a pretty) **photographer** (named Jackie Bouvier)
- (1953: Jack and Jackie were) **married**
- (1954: severe back) **pain** (led to an operation)
- (1954: after back operation) **infection** (set in and was nearly fatal)
- (1955: after) **recuperation** (he returned to Washington)
- (1955: had another book published, *Profiles in*) **Courage**
- (1957: won) **Pulitzer** (Prize for his book)
- (1957: baby) **Carolyn** (born)
- (1960: baby) **John** (born)
- (1961: Jack) **inaugurated** (president)

B	W	D	H	K	O	E	Q	C	S	D	G	A
I	O	P	T	W	N	A	U	C	E	Y	R	W
F	R	I	N	F	E	C	T	I	O	N	D	A
N	K	J	V	B	L	E	R	H	E	Y	M	S
G	E	F	J	L	N	R	M	G	K	L	I	H
P	D	W	Q	P	A	R	A	N	H	O	J	I
H	O	U	S	M	W	R	E	T	V	R	S	N
O	B	G	C	P	U	D	T	F	A	A	Y	G
T	I	K	A	O	A	N	A	M	J	C	H	T
O	L	P	C	E	R	P	N	U	S	Q	O	O
G	T	C	O	N	G	R	E	S	S	M	A	N
R	W	A	D	I	C	X	S	R	E	Y	B	V
A	J	L	H	A	G	N	U	Y	R	I	M	F
P	Z	Q	O	P	U	L	I T	Z	E	R	Z
H	W	D	E	T	A	R	U	G	U	A	N	I
E	P	D	L	R	S	G	N	K	T	O	J	F
R	E	C	U	P	E	R	A	T	I	O	N	H

104

John F. Kennedy
1961–1963

SKYSCRAPER
DIRECTIONS
Write your answers in the boxes. The circled letters will help you.

1. Abbr. for birth state: _____
2. His famous words: "Ask not what your country can do for you; ask what _____ can do for your country."
3. 1961: The Peace _____ was created.
4. Foreign aid sent to _____ and Africa for starving people.
5. 1961: first American astronaut: _____ Shepherd
6. Americans walked on the _____.
7. 1961: The Berlin _____ was built. (divider)
8. 1962: evidence of Russian missiles in _____ (island country)
9. 1962: Kennedy ordered a blockade of Russian _____ in Cuba.
10. 1962: In a blockade, Russian ships were _____; war was averted. (halted)
11. 1964: The Civil _____ Act became law.
12. 1963: Campaigning in _____, he was shot. (state)
13. Vice-Pres. _____ was inaugurated pres.

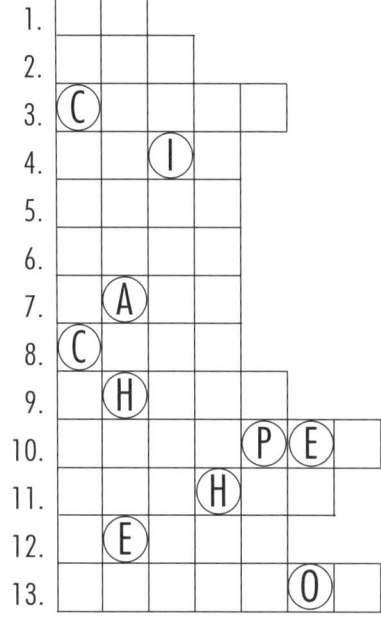

CLUE
DIRECTIONS
Each set of lines has vowels and an occasional consonant to help you determine the correct answer. All the words tell about John F. Kennedy.

1. Born: __ a __ 29, 1917
2. As a child, he had scarlet __ e __ e __.
3. As a child, he had chicken __ o __.
4. While ill in bed, he liked to __ e a __.
5. As a young man, he liked winning at s __ o __ __ __.
6. Jack and a friend, Lem, __ a i __ e __ to Europe to visit.
7. Joseph took his family to live in __ o __ __ o __, England, where he worked.
8. Carolyn Kennedy had a __ o __ y called Macaroni.
9. Kennedy was buried in A __ __ i __ __ __ o __ National Cemetery.
10. World __ e a __ e __ __ attended the funeral.
11. At his funeral, 51 __ __ a __ e __ flew overhead and 21 rifles fired in a __ a __ u __ e.

105

Lyndon B. Johnson
1963–1969

CROSSWORD PUZZLE

ACROSS

1. Pres. Roosevelt started NYA (National Youth Administration) to give young _____ part-time jobs.
3. Lyndon and Lady Bird were _____. (wed)
6. As a man, he _____ his childhood ranch. (purchased)
8. 1930 Great Depression: _____ were scarce, but he taught at a Houston high school.
9. Birth state: _____
11. Father's occupations: rancher and school _____
14. 1934: He met Claudia Taylor, nicknamed "Lady _____."
15. The Johnsons owned a _____. (large cattle farm)
17. Had three _____ and one brother.
19. Childhood chore: chopping firewood and _____ it
20. Worked very _____ at every job he had.
23. 1931: In Washington, he worked for a _____ from TX. (politician)
26. 1937: At 28, was elected to _____ of Representatives.
27. 1941: Japan _____ Pearl Harbor, Hawaii.
29. 1942: Roosevelt called Lyndon to _____. (capital)
30. 1941: Lyndon was Lt. Commander in U.S. _____.

DOWN

2. Father: Elected to the state _____ five times.
4. Born: _____ 27, 1908.

5. At 3, Lyndon could spell some words and _____ simple stories.
7. Mother's name: _____
10. College: Was excellent at _____. (arguing issues)
12. Ranch animals: _____, chickens, donkeys
13. Lyndon rode a _____ to school. (animal)
16. At six, Lyndon moved with parents to Johnson _____, TX.
18. After two years in college, he taught _____.
21. Washington: Was a _____ for a congressman.
22. Was _____ of NYA in TX. (chief)
24. 1955: Lyndon had a _____ attack.
25. Father's name: _____
28. Lyndon, 15, was _____ feet, 3 inches tall.

Lyndon B. Johnson
1963–1969

SUPPLY THE VOWEL
DIRECTIONS
In the grid, look for the following words (the words that are not in parentheses). The words can go up, down, across, at angles, backward, or forward. Parts of words may overlap. Supply the correct vowel—a e i o u—for the center of each word group.

(1944:) **baby** (Lynda, born)
(1947: baby) **Luci** (born)
(1948: campaigned for Senate in a) **helicopter**
(1953:) **Eisenhower** (inaugurated pres.)
(1961: Kennedy was pres; Lyndon) **vice** (-pres.)
(1963: Kennedy shot by an) **assassin**
(1963: Lyndon Johnson inaugurated as) **president**

B	A	H	L	S	M	P	P	E	O	S	P	B
D	L	N	W	R	J	T	W	U	H	R	V	Q
Y	B	○	B	N	Y	L	C	Y	○	A	R	A
C	L	S	C	B	F	H	F	S	L	B	G	D
I	L	S	E	K	N	D	I	M	I	P	L	J
S	V	A	R	U	S	D	Y	T	C	A	W	O
K	B	S	D	H	E	K	J	F	O	G	C	O
N	R	S	O	N	Y	S	P	M	P	R	W	L
U	A	I	T	P	O	○	R	V	T	E	Y	S
T	D	N	C	G	L	C	U	F	E	W	B	E
I	Y	L	N	D	H	I	O	N	R	O	K	R
M	L	T	E	S	V	E	W	U	G	H	J	P
C	P	R	I	B	E	T	L	H	D	N	G	A
C	P	C	K	J	M	Y	P	I	O	E	F	E
R	○	N	N	Y	D	S	A	R	V	S	C	L
L	S	B	C	F	M	I	H	T	X	○	S	Q
T	B	H	A	V	J	G	E	W	V	E	C	U

(1963: Johnson, thirty-)**sixth** (pres.)
(1964:) **Civil** (Rights laws passed)
(1964: passage of two Civil Rights) **laws** (for desegregation and against discrimination)
(laws passed to help) **poor**
(1964: Johnson had plans for a Great) **Society**
(1964: Head Start began for) **young** (children)
(1964: Medicare began for) **older** (people)
(1964: Castro wanted U.S. out of) **Cuba** (and cut off a U.S. base's water supply)
(1964: U.S. captured Cuban fishing boats and planned to fire Cuban employees at U.S. base; water) **supply** (came back on)
(1965: laws guaranteed voting rights for) **blacks**
(1968: N. Korea captured U.S.S.) *Pueblo*
(1968: *Pueblo* crew held about one) **year**
(1968: Lyndon did not) **run** (for pres. again)

107

Lyndon B. Johnson
1963–1969

NAME THE HELICOPTER

DIRECTIONS

Fill in the dotted lines with your answers. If they are correct, the circled letters will spell the name of the helicopter that carried Lyndon Johnson around Texas while he campaigned for the U.S. Senate. "Johnson . . ." is the first word. Supply the other words.

1. First African American Supreme _____ judge: Thurgood Marshall
2. Lyndon's wife: Lady _____ Johnson
3. Bitter civil war: North and _____ Korea
4. Pres. _____ was shot in Dallas, TX.
5. Johnson was inaugurated president in *Air _____ One.* (plane)
6. _____ Kennedy attended the inauguration.
7. John _____, governor of TX, was shot also.
8. Secret _____ men did not want parade route known.
9. Parade route was published in the _____.
10. Johnson took nitro_____ pills for heart pain.
11. Johnson and his _____ owned a broadcasting company.
12. _____ Kennedy was taken to a Dallas hospital.
13. Hearing gunshots, people screamed and _____.
14. When Kennedy died, _____ became president.
15. _____ Luther King was assassinated.
16. Secret Service men guard all _____.
17. After retiring, _____ returned to his ranch.
18. _____ died in 1973.

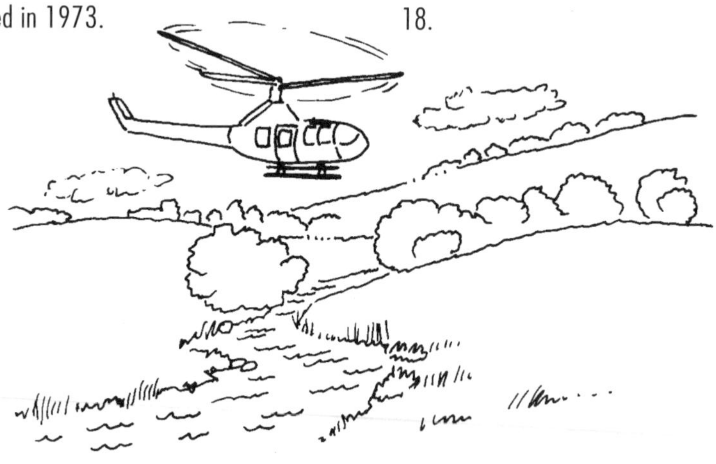

108

Richard M. Nixon
1969–1974

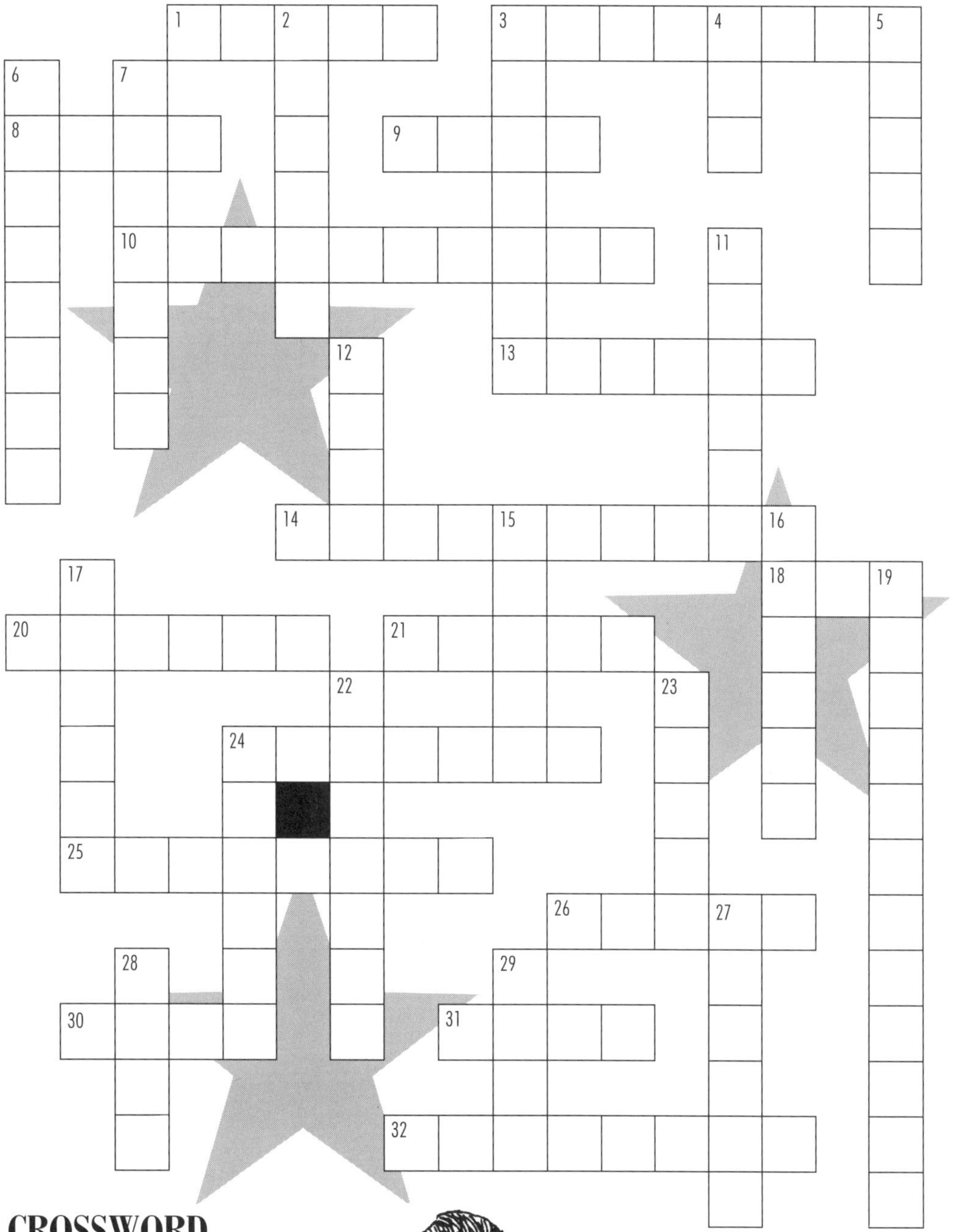

CROSSWORD PUZZLE

ACROSS

1. His grandfather died in the _____ War. (at Gettysburg)
3. Father's ancestors: _____ (country)
8. At 3, Richard fell from horse-drawn buggy: deep cut on _____.
9. Met teacher, Pat Ryan, and fell in _____.
10. Birth state: _____
13. Mother's name: _____
14. At 6, Richard read _____ and talked about news with his father.
18. Wife's name: _____
20. In grade 11, he wanted to be a _____. (profession)
21. Father's name: _____
24. Father: Opened a gas and service _____; was successful.
25. Eighth grade: excellent at _____ (arguing issues)
26. Was up at 4:00 A.M. to get _____ food for father's store. (not stale)
30. Hannah made _____ to sell. (a pastry)
31. Richard worked at odd _____ to help the family.
32. Went to law school in North _____. (state)

DOWN

2. Played a _____ in school. (stringed instrument)
3. Nixon: thirty-_____ pres.
4. 1937: Graduated from _____ school.
5. Hannah's Quaker family did not _____ alcohol.
6. Nixons lived in _____, CA, a quiet Quaker town with orange trees.
7. Hannah's family allowed no _____ or music.
11. Hannah was a quiet _____ woman. (denomination)
12. Pat's mother died; Pat, 14, took _____ of the family.
15. Richard played the _____ very well. (keyboard)
16. He participated in _____ in high school. (athletics)
17. Brother _____ died.
19. Harold died of _____. (lung disease)
22. Nixon later became excellent at dealing with foreign _____. (countries)
23. Father opened a successful general _____. (selling things)
24. 1800s: Hannah's family aided runaway _____.
27. Graduated _____ in his college class. (next to top)
28. Brother Arthur _____.
29. Had _____ brothers.

109

Richard M. Nixon
1969–1974

CROSSING OVER

DIRECTIONS

Use a pencil for this game. Using the words that are not in parentheses, find words from the following list that have the correct number of spaces and letters to fit into the crossing-over boxes. Each word has a place where it belongs. The first word is done for you. To continue, find a seven-letter word with an "n" in the fourth space. All the words tell about Richard M. Nixon.

3 letters

Pat (worked hard)

(Richard got a) job (in Washington)

(1969: Nixon said he wanted the Vietnam War to) end

4 letters

(1941: Japan bombed Pearl Harbor; Nixon joined U.S.) Navy

(1960: Kennedy pres.; Nixon) lost (the election)

(1968: civil rights leader Martin Luther) King (was killed)

5 letters

(1948: daughter) Julie (was born)

(1957: a) black (girl entered a white high school in the South; gov't troops guarded her)

(1968:) Nixon (inaugurated pres.)

6 letters

(got) awards (for good schoolwork)

(father pleased with Richard's) report (cards)

(Pat worked in) fields (to help her father)

(1946: daughter) Tricia (was born)

(Nixon helped send spy, Alger Hiss, to) prison

(1950: elected to U.S.) Senate

(Eisenhower had a heart) attack

(communism seemed a dangerous) threat

7 letters

(born) January (9, 1913)

(1940: Richard and Pat) married

(1963: Pres.) Kennedy (was killed)

(1975: N. Vietnam took over S.) Vietnam

(Nixon met with) leaders (in Africa)

8 letters

(Nixon's dog's name:) Checkers

(1946: elected to) Congress

(Marshall Plan: helped) starving (Europeans)

(1968: Julie Nixon married Eisenhower's) grandson

(Nixon saw) horrible (Berlin Wall)

9 letters

(Vice Pres. Nixon visited many) countries

10 letters

(1941: the Nixons moved to) Washington

(1941: was) Lieutenant (in U.S. Navy)

(1953:) Eisenhower (pres.; Nixon, vice-pres.)

Richard M. Nixon
1969–1974

PAIRS

DIRECTIONS

All of the Richard M. Nixon words in the large box are written twice, except for one. Write the name of each Nixon pair on a line. (Cross off the pairs as you find them.) Then find the word that appears only once, and write it in the box.

NUMBER CODE

DIRECTIONS

Look at the numbers under each line. Find the matching numbers in the code box, and write the letters on the corresponding answer lines.

1. In 1974, Richard Nixon became the only president who ever __ __ __ __ __ __ __ __
   18 5 19 9 7 14 5 4

   __ __ __ __ __ __ __ __ __ __ .
   6 18 15 13   15 6 6 9 3 5

2. The House Judiciary Committee reviewed evidence and __ __ __ __ __ __ __ __ __ __
   18 5 3 15 13 13 5 14 4 5 4

   __ __ __ __ __ __ __ __ __ __ __ . The reasons were obstructing
   9 13 16 5 1 3 8 9 14 7   8 9 13

   __ __ __ __ __ __ __ ; abusing __ __ __ __ __ __ __ __ __ __ __ __
   10 21 19 20 9 3 5   16 18 5 19 9 4 5 14 20 9 1 12

   power; and disobeying __ __ __ __ __ __ __ __ __ .
                         19 21 2 16 15 5 14 1 19

3. He faced __ __ __ __ __ __ __ __ __ __ __ __ __ __ impeachment, so he
            1 12 13 15 19 20   3 5 18 20 1 9 14

   __ __ __ __ __ __ __ __ .
   18 5 19 9 7 14 5 4

A - 1	N - 14
B - 2	O - 15
C - 3	P - 16
D - 4	Q - 17
E - 5	R - 18
F - 6	S - 19
G - 7	T - 20
H - 8	U - 21
I - 9	V - 22
J - 10	W - 23
K - 11	X - 24
L - 12	Y - 25
M - 13	Z - 26

Gerald R. Ford
1974–1977

CROSSWORD PUZZLE

ACROSS

1. Stepfather, Gerald Ford, Sr., adopted him; changed his _____ from Leslie King to Gerald Ford, Jr.
3. At birth, Gerald (Jerry) was given the name _____.
5. Boyhood chore: cutting the _____.
7. Mother's name: _____
8. He had a coaching job at _____ University while studying law. (in CT)
9. 1915: Dorothy and Leslie King _____ and were divorced. (parted)
11. Dorothy then married _____ Ford, Sr.
13. Gerald, Jr., was nicknamed _____.
14. Worked hard in _____. (place of learning)
16. He was both right- and _____-handed.
20. Got good _____ in school.
21. He was _____ of the state champion football team.
22. Favorite school subjects: _____ and government (the past)
24. As a boy: _____-working
25. Fell in love with Betty; they were _____.
26. 1950: Baby _____ was born.
27. Played _____ football at University of Michigan.

DOWN

1. Birth state: _____
2. Boyhood chore: cleaning the _____.
4. Became an _____ Scout
6. Liked _____. (athletics)
10. Dorothy had _____ more sons with Mr. Ford.
11. His stepfather taught him _____ morals.
12. High school: Washed _____ and waited tables.
15. The Fords went to _____. (religious place)
17. Played championship _____ in high school.
18. He got pro football offers from Green Bay _____ and Detroit Lions.
19. Played winning football at University of _____.
23. Was in an airplane crash but _____.
28. 1942: Joined the _____ as an ensign.

112

Gerald R. Ford
1974–1977

WORD SEARCHING
DIRECTIONS
In the grid, find these words about Gerald Ford (the words that are not in parentheses). They can go up, down, across, at an angle, forward, or backward.

B	U	I	L	D	I	N	G	D	C	U	B	A
D	C	F	J	E	A	J	L	K	H	B	I	G
N	P	O	C	U	V	U	W	S	T	Y	R	M
A	E	M	O	D	E	L	D	B	G	R	H	C
R	I	K	N	P	J	Y	F	O	E	M	L	N
E	R	V	G	T	Y	U	Z	D	W	A	T	S
I	B	D	R	C	W	G	A	F	H	S	E	A
R	K	I	E	N	J	E	M	G	L	S	S	R
R	V	O	S	U	L	W	N	T	P	A	R	E
A	B	E	S	D	C	O	I	T	A	S	Y	W
C	N	F	I	J	R	L	X	H	Y	S	G	O
P	R	O	T	T	K	S	O	N	U	I	M	H
A	Y	E	S	C	G	B	N	D	W	N	P	N
H	M	J	I	N	L	P	O	K	F	A	O	E
S	W	A	E	L	H	U	N	V	R	T	R	S
Y	T	G	M	F	K	O	D	H	B	E	S	I
K	E	N	N	E	D	Y	J	C	J	D	N	E

(for a while, Jerry was a) **model** (for a magazine)

(he was an officer on the aircraft) **carrier** (U.S.S. *Monterey*)

(he campaigned for a seat in) **Congress**

(was in Congress for) **twenty** (-five years)

(Jerry wanted a) **strong** (America)

(he was in the same office) **building** (as Kennedy and Nixon)

(1953: Jerry helped get) **Eisenhower** (elected pres.)

(1960:) **Kennedy** (was elected president)

(1962: U.S. spy planes discovered Russian nuclear missiles in) **Cuba**

(1963: Pres. Kennedy was) **assassinated**

(1963:) **Johnson** (became president)

(1965: Jerry became House Minority) **Leader**

(1964:) **Nixon** (was inaugurated president)

(Jerry was born) **July** (14, 1913)

113

Gerald R. Ford
1974–1977

SCRAMBLED WORDS
DIRECTIONS
Unscramble the words and write the answers on the lines provided. (Use scrap paper to work out your answers.)

1. People were angry about the war in NEVMAIT. _____
2. 1972: Five men broke into the Democratic Headquarters at the AEAGTWTRE Hotel to plant listening devices. _____
3. 1972: Nixon aides were put in OSRPNI for criminal acts. _____
4. Ford believed Nixon was not IUGLYT. _____
5. Vice-Pres. NWAGE resigned for wrongdoing. _____
6. 1973: Jerry Ford was RONSW in as vice-pres. _____
7. People wanted to MAHICEP Nixon for wrongdoing. _____
8. Ford began to SUINOTQE Nixon's innocence. _____
9. Nixon was ordered by the Supreme Court to provide SPTEA of his conversations with his aides. _____
10. The Court discovered vital parts of the tapes had been SDEEAR. _____
11. Nixon EESNRIGD so he wouldn't be impeached. _____

SKYSCRAPER
DIRECTIONS
Write your answers in the boxes. The circled letters will help you.

1. Initials for the state where Ford was born: _____
2. The city where he was born: _____
3. 1974: Nixon resigned and _____ became president.
4. Ford pardoned Nixon from all _____ doing, which made people angry.
5. Ford tried hard to do what was _____ for the country.
6. N. Vietnam didn't keep its promise not to _____ S. Vietnam.
7. Ford performed well as pres. and kept the _____ together.
8. Two _____ tried to shoot Ford.
9. 1977: _____ was inaugurated pres.
10. 1977: Betty and Jerry moved to _____. (state)
11. 1979: Jerry wrote a book about his life and _____.

Circled letters in grid:
2. H
4. G
5. E
6. D
8. O, E
9. E
10. A, I
11. C

114

James E. Carter, Jr.
1977–1981

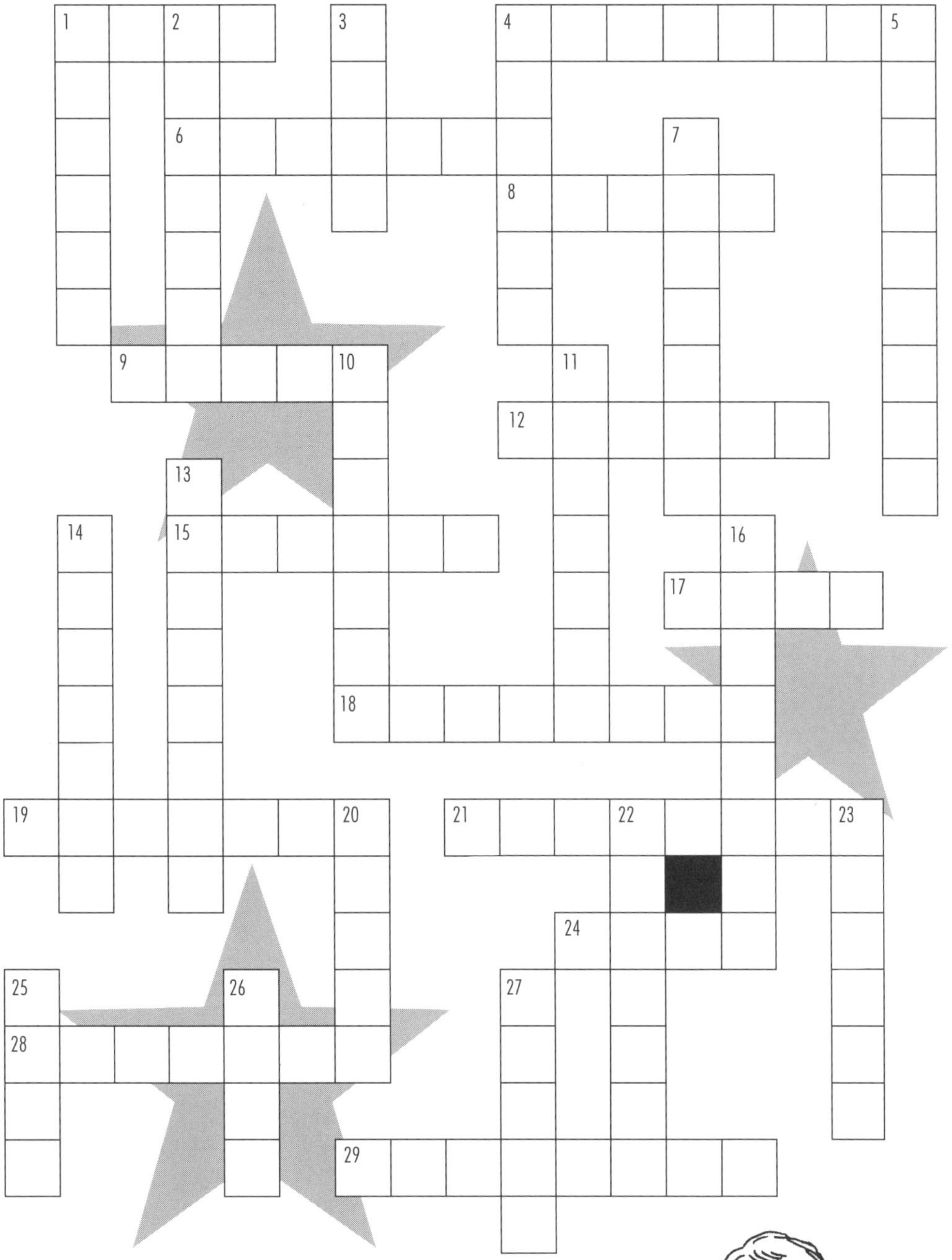

CROSSWORD PUZZLE

ACROSS

1. Boyhood chore: gathering _____ (poultry)
4. Mother, Lillian, made comforters from soft goose _____.
6. Born: _____ 1, 1924
8. Farm wagons were pulled by _____. (stubborn animals)
9. Father's name: _____
12. At 6, Jimmy sold peanuts in town when he wasn't working in the _____. (planted areas)
15. Water for baths had to be _____. (warmed)
17. The Carters worked _____. (diligently)
18. Home was on the road between _____ and Columbus, GA.
19. Farm crops: _____, cotton, corn
21. Farm crops: white potatoes, sweet _____, watermelons
24. Great Depression: Carters had food from their _____.
28. Jimmy took flying _____.
29. He met a pretty girl, _____, and fell in love.

DOWN

1. 1941: World War II began in _____. (continent)
2. Birthplace: Plains, _____
3. Boyhood chore: chopping _____
4. Father's occupations: _____ and owner of a farm store
5. 1948: Jimmy was assigned to _____ duty at sea.
7. Boyhood chore: killing boll _____ (cotton insects)
10. Had two _____ and one brother.
11. Mother's name: Bessie Lillian, called _____
13. Farm animals: _____ (poultry)
14. 1946: Jimmy and Rosalynn were _____. (wed)
16. Carter farm had no indoor _____. (for bathing and toilet)
20. In the war he identified enemy _____ and planes.
22. Was appointed to U.S. Naval _____ at Annapolis.
23. He went to a one-room _____.
25. In WW II he _____ seaplanes. (maneuvered)
26. 1948: Baby _____ was born.
27. 1946: Graduated from the _____ Academy.

115

James E. Carter, Jr.
1977–1981

SUPPLY THE VOWEL

DIRECTIONS

In the grid, look for the following words (the words that are not in parentheses). The words can go up, down, across, at angles, backward, or forward. Parts of words may overlap. Supply the correct vowel—a e i o u—for the center of each word group.

C	H	S	R	G	O	B	N	J	A	D	E	I
L	S	T	N	S	K	F	P	M	V	I	L	M
E	D	○	C	A	T	I	O	N	O	E	P	W
Y	R	N	C	E	B	L	D	L	U	N	O	J
C	F	A	H	C	N	G	C	L	R	A	○	R
I	M	E	O	S	E	K	V	R	J	F	P	Y
T	A	P	W	U	C	S	B	Y	F	C	P	A
E	I	R	H	R	T	K	S	Y	O	D	M	K
S	G	E	D	U	F	N	S	P	M	R	C	L
F	A	C	C	H	J	E	D	E	B	○	T	E
D	J	I	W	L	N	G	B	K	J	H	E	V
S	U	F	S	A	O	Y	N	Y	I	L	P	M
W	T	F	T	D	H	F	A	M	R	N	T	J
D	R	○	W	N	E	D	K	M	P	K	B	M
U	R	E	V	P	R	E	S	○	D	E	N	T
B	W	O	T	E	G	A	H	J	N	S	R	C
P	C	V	Y	H	G	C	J	E	I	D	D	F

(mother, Lillian, cooked on a wood-burning) **stove**

(8th grade: Jimmy learned to) **debate** (issues)

(main farm crop:) **peanuts**

(Jimmy was very) **kind** (to poor workers)

(he became senior) **officer** (on a submarine)

(once he nearly) **drowned** (at sea)

(Jimmy's birth name: James) **Earl** (Carter)

(Jimmy believed that black children and white children should have an equal) **education**

(he didn't want black) **people** (kept out of his church)

(Jimmy resigned from the U.S. Navy to) **run** (Father's peanut business)

(Jimmy and Rosalynn worked) **hard** (on the peanut farm)

(peanut farm was a) **success**

(baby John's nickname was) **Jack**

(baby Donnell Jeffrey was called) **Jeff**

(baby James was nicknamed) **Chip**

(1962: he won a seat as State) **Senator**

(as Senator, he worked hard to save Georgia) **money**

(1967: baby) **Amy** (was born)

(1970:) **Jimmy** (was Georgia's governor)

(1974: he ran for) **president** (and won)

Presidential Puzzlers Copyright © 2005 Good Year Books

James E. Carter, Jr.
1977–1981

NAME THE GROUP THAT WORKED HARD TO ELECT CARTER PRESIDENT

DIRECTIONS

Fill in the dotted lines with your answers. If they are correct, the circled letters will spell the name of the group that worked hard to elect Carter president.

1. 1971: Gov. Jimmy Carter's _____ was on the front of *Time* magazine; as a southerner in favor of desegregation.
2. 1971: Was chairman of the National _____ Party Campaign Committee.
3. 1974: _____, with his family, announced he would run for president.
4. Jimmy had a _____ for his campaign. (goal)
5. One campaign worker went to each state and got the Democratic Party to invite Jimmy to speak and answer _____.
6. Carter did _____ spend a lot of campaign money.

7. On a cold January 4, campaign workers, with _____ on their feet, paying their own way, visited Democratic voters in NH to ask for votes for Jimmy.
8. Newspapers and TV reported about Carter. He later won the New Hampshire _____.
9. He won the primaries in _____, Maine, Vermont, Iowa, Oklahoma, and Wisconsin.
10. Carter's campaign poster at the Democratic Convention showed a big _____ peanut, representing his smile. (smiling)
11. Carter chose Walter _____ as his running mate.
12. Jimmy Carter and Gerald Ford had _____ on TV. (arguments)
13. 1977: Carter was inaugurated _____.

1. _ _ O _ _ _
2. _ O _ _ _ _ _ _ _
3. _ O _ _ _ _
4. _ _ O _
5. _ O _ _ _ _ _ _
6. _ O _
7. _ O _ _ _
8. _ O _ _ _ _ _
9. _ _ O _ _
10. _ O _ _ _ _ _
11. _ _ _ O _ _
12. _ O _ _ _ _ _
13. _ _ O _ _ _ _ _

NUMBER CODE

DIRECTIONS

Look at the numbers under each line. Find the matching numbers in the code box, and write the letters on the corresponding answer lines.

1. On TV, Pres. Carter talked to the American __ __ __ __ __ __
   16 5 15 16 12 5

   as he sat by a __ __ __ __ __ __ __ __ __ in the White House.
   6 9 18 5 16 12 1 3 5

2. President Carter wanted jobs for the unemployed, help for the
   __ __ __ __, __ __ __ __ __ __ pollution, and water conservation.
   16 15 15 18   12 15 23 5 18

3. Carter met with leaders of __ __ __ __ __ __ and __ __ __ __ __
   9 19 18 1 5 12   5 7 25 16 20

   at Camp David, to work out differences.

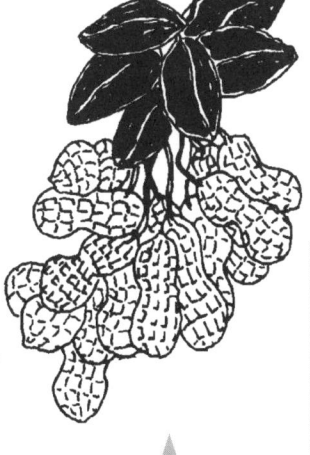
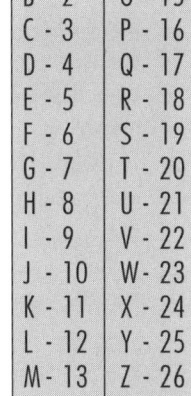

A - 1	N - 14
B - 2	O - 15
C - 3	P - 16
D - 4	Q - 17
E - 5	R - 18
F - 6	S - 19
G - 7	T - 20
H - 8	U - 21
I - 9	V - 22
J - 10	W - 23
K - 11	X - 24
L - 12	Y - 25
M - 13	Z - 26

Ronald W. Reagan
1981–1989

CROSSWORD PUZZLE

ACROSS

3. Ronald liked to collect bird _____. (in nests)
6. Birthplace: Tampico, _____.
7. As a young man, he became a famous movie _____.
8. Mother's name: _____
10. Father had a _____ problem and had trouble keeping a job. (alcoholic)
14. Ronald loved playing _____. (sport)
16. 1929: Great Depression began in the U.S.; people were _____. (wanted food)
17. He needed _____ to see better.
22. Met actress _____ Wyman, and they got married.
25. Liked _____ in school plays. (performing)
26. 1942: Was drafted into the _____.
27. He was tall, _____, and cheerful. (good looks)
29. Got a job as a _____ announcer. (for listening)
31. 1948: He and Jane got a _____. (separated)

DOWN

1. His mother was kind and was always _____ others in need.
2. Liked high school sports: football, _____, track.
4. To grow _____, got a job digging with a pick axe.
5. Father's name: _____
9. Ancestors were from _____. (country)
10. Ronald's nickname: _____
11. Mother read _____ to her boys every night.
12. As an actor, he learned his _____ quickly.
13. 1941: Japan bombed Pearl _____, Hawaii.
15. 1933: As a lifeguard, he put notches on a _____ for each person he rescued. (tree part)
18. An excellent swimmer, he got a job as a _____ at the river. (rescuer)
19. 1932: Graduated from college and wanted to act in _____. (movies)
20. Wanted to be a _____ star.
21. 1941: Baby _____ was born to Jane.
23. To pay for college, he worked on campus _____ dishes, shoveling snow, raking leaves.
24. In the army reserve, he rode horses in the _____. (mounted troops)
28. He took a _____ test for movies.
30. Due to poor eyesight, he was given a job narrating films to _____ aerial gunners. (prepare)

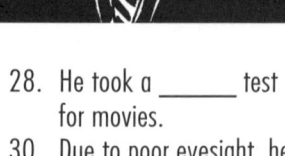

118

Ronald W. Reagan
1981–1989

CROSSING OVER
DIRECTIONS
Use a pencil for this game. Using the words that are not in parentheses, find words from the following list that have the correct number of spaces and letters to fit into the crossing-over boxes. Each word has a place where it belongs. The first word is done for you. To continue, find a seven-letter word having an "n" in the fifth space. All the words tell about Ronald Reagan.

2 letters
(initials for birth state) IL

3 letters
(had) one (brother)

4 letters
(1967: he got CA out of) debt
(1967: took) oath (as gov. of CA)
(1981: a gunman) shot (Reagan; he recovered)

5 letters
(Ronald met actress) Nancy (Davis)
(he) dated (Nancy and later married her)

(1948: first wife, Jane, got an) Oscar (for acting)
(1952: baby) Patti (was born)
(1962: gave more than 200 campaign speeches for) Nixon
(as gov. saved CA) money
(was CA governor) eight (years)
(As pres., he shared jelly) beans (at Cabinet meetings)
(1970: was gov.) again
(he bought a horse) ranch

6 letters
(1965: hosted a TV western series, "Death) Valley (Days")
(1977: Carter (became pres.)
(1958: baby) Ronald (born to Nancy)
(1981) Reagan (became pres.)
(1960s: as gov., he sent troops to stop) campus (riots)

7 letters
(1954: was host of TV show, "The General Electric) Theater (")
(1960s: college students rioted against war in) Vietnam
(1981: Sandra Day O'Connor was first woman) Supreme (Court Justice)
(national debt grew) rapidly (while he was pres.)
(Ronald and Jane adopted baby) Michael

8 letters
(Ronald became interested in) politics
(ran for) governor (of CA)
(Nixon) resigned (due to Watergate)
(1981: Ronald cut gov't) spending
(college: was captain of) swimming (team)

9 letters
(Americans feared) communism
(Nixon resigned; Ford was) president

11 letters
(1981: Reagan fired striking air traffic) controllers

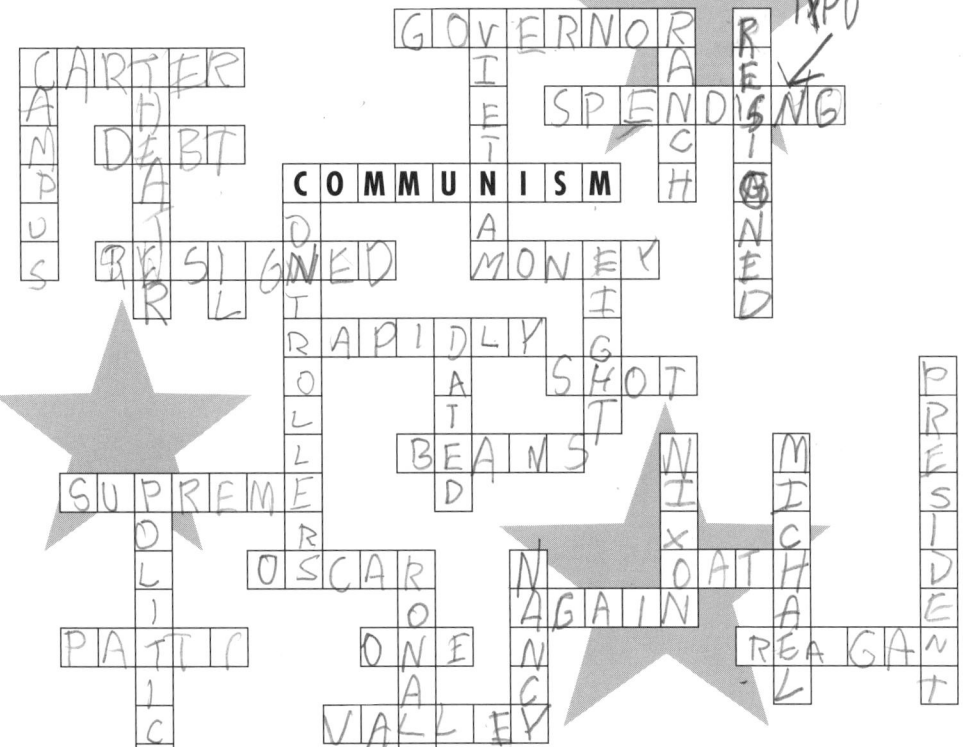

Ronald W. Reagan
1981–1989

PAIRS
DIRECTIONS
All of the Ronald Reagan words in the large box are written twice, except for one. Write the name of each pair on a line. (Cross off the pairs as you find them.) Then find the name of the Reagan word that appears only once, and write it in the box.

Word box contains: Beirut, killed, Marines, Kaddafi, Grenada, Communists, Kuwait, NASA, Beirut, Persian Gulf, Grenada, astronauts, Libya, explosion, oil, beaches, rescue, beaches, students, terrorists, oil, Marines, paratroopers, space, students, Persian Gulf, paratroopers, rescue, killed, explosion, Libya, Challenger, Communists, space, Iran, Iraq, Communists, Kuwait, NASA, terrorists, Kaddafi, astronauts

CLUE
DIRECTIONS
Each set of lines has vowels and an occasional consonant to help you determine the correct answer. All the words tell about Ronald Reagan.

1. 1980s: Nancy Reagan's campaign slogan against   d __ u __ __ : " J u __ __ __ a __ __ o."

2. 1985: Reagan was inaugurated again as pres.; __ e o __ __ e __ u __ __ as vice-pres.

3. Libyan terrorist leader __ a __ __ a __ i gave Arabs __ u __ __ to attack U.S. citizens.

4. In retaliation, the U.S. __ o __ __ e d Libya.

5. 1985: Trouble erupted in the __ e __ __ i a __ G u __ __ between Iraq and Iran.

6. 1985: Ronald had an o __ e __ a __ i o __ for c a __ __ e __ .

7. 1986: NASA space flight C h a __ __ e __ __ e __ e __ __ __ o __ e __ in the air, killing all aboard.

8. Reagan and Russian leader __ o __ __ a __ __ e __ worked toward limiting nuclear arms.

9. 1989: __ u __ __ was inaugurated pres.

10. 1989: Ronald and Nancy moved back to __ a __ i __ o __ __ i a.

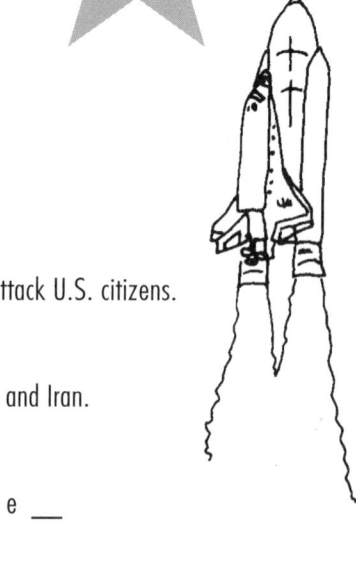

120

George H. W. Bush
1989–1993

31. 1941: George and Barbara were secretly _____. (a promise)

DOWN

1. At 18: He was in the U.S. Navy; preflight training for _____. (conflict)
2. Father's name: _____
4. Father moved family to _____, CT.
5. George loved all kinds of _____. (athletics)
7. Parents taught their children strong _____ values. (honorable)
8. As a teen he was over 6 _____ tall.
10. George treated _____ fairly. (people)
12. Mother's name: _____
14. George arrived home on _____ Eve, 1944.
17. At 18: Was youngest U.S. Navy _____. (flyer)
18. Flew _____-eight combat missions in war.
20. Was an _____ student at Yale U. (outstanding)
21. He won _____ for outstanding bravery in war.
25. He painted Barbara's name on _____ he flew.
27. 1949: Baby _____ was born.
28. Mother, Dorothy, won every foot_____ she entered. (contest)

CROSSWORD PUZZLE

ACROSS

3. Christmas 1941, George met _____.
6. January 1945: He and Barbara were _____.
7. Birth state: _____
9. Parents used discipline and _____ with their children. (affection)
11. He willingly _____ what he had with others.
13. George moved his family to TX to work in the _____ fields.
15. Had _____ brothers and one sister.
16. Dec. 7, 1941: Japan bombed Pearl _____.
18. Was a soccer star, for he was very _____.
19. Was well-liked in _____. (place of learning)
22. Was on active _____ in the Pacific Ocean on a torpedo bomber squadron.
23. 1945: _____ bomb dropped on Japan; war ended.
24. Parents had servants: chauffeur, _____, and cook.
26. 1945: He attended _____ University in CT.
29. 1944: His plane was shot down, and he was rescued by a _____. (underwater ship)
30. _____ June 1924

121

George H. W. Bush
1989–1993

WORD SEARCHING

DIRECTIONS

In the grid, find these words about George Bush (the words that are not in parentheses). They can go up, down, across, at an angle, forward, or backward.

(1946: baby) **George** (born)

(George learned the oil) **business** (in TX)

(1950s: he started his own oil-producing) **company**

(1953: Robin, nearly 4, died of) **leukemia**

(1953: because of anxiety about Robin's illness, Barbara's hair quickly turned from brown to) **white**

(1953: baby) **John** (born; nicknamed Jeb)

(1955: baby) **Neil** (born)

(1956: baby) **Marvin** (born)

(1959: baby) **Dorothy** (born)

(1967: George was in U.S.) **Congress**

(while Congressman, George and family invited many people to Sunday evening) **barbecues**

(Pres. Nixon appointed George Ambassador to the United) **Nations**

(Pres. Ford sent George and Barbara to China and they bicycled around Beijing, smiled, and learned the) **language**

(1975: George was made CIA) **director** (in U.S.)

(1980: Reagan asked George to be his) **vice** (-pres.)

J	B	F	E	H	D	I	S	C	G	C	A	D
K	O	M	P	N	L	S	C	O	L	O	J	O
S	U	H	W	T	E	Y	L	M	A	V	R	R
D	G	B	N	N	U	F	A	P	E	H	C	O
J	S	M	I	N	K	L	N	A	K	D	I	T
R	E	S	N	T	E	P	G	N	E	I	L	H
W	U	V	A	S	M	Y	U	Y	U	R	O	Y
B	C	D	T	C	I	E	A	B	G	E	F	A
I	E	K	I	M	A	O	G	J	N	C	L	H
R	B	T	O	S	W	V	E	Y	U	T	P	S
C	R	B	N	H	L	G	T	J	D	O	A	S
M	A	U	S	E	R	E	O	T	G	R	N	E
C	B	I	A	F	Y	O	H	B	N	D	W	R
G	P	J	L	M	A	R	V	I	N	S	E	G
V	I	C	E	N	P	G	A	H	V	I	K	N
R	U	B	O	S	D	E	F	K	M	O	E	O
W	H	I	T	E	I	M	T	L	C	G	W	C

122

George H. W. Bush
1989–1993

NUMBER CODE
DIRECTIONS
Look at the numbers under each line. Find the matching numbers in the code box, and write the letters on the corresponding answer lines.

1. 1981: Pres. Reagan sent George on peace visits to 59 __ __ __ __ __ __ __ __ __ .
   3 15 21 14 20 18 9 5 19

2. 1989: Exxon ship *Valdez* spilled huge amounts of oil in __ __ __ __ __ __ .
   1 12 1 19 11 1

3. 1989: Bush was inaugurated __ __ __ __ __ __ __ __ __ ; Quayle was vice-president.
   16 18 5 19 9 4 5 14 20

4. 1989: He had a big plan for war on __ __ __ __ __ .
   4 18 21 7 19

5. 1989: The Berlin __ __ __ __ was taken down.
   23 1 12 12

6. 1989: U.S. soldiers landed at __ __ __ __ __ __ .
   16 1 14 1 13 1

7. 1990: Panama's military leader, Manuel __ __ __ __ __ __ __ , surrendered to the U.S.
   14 15 18 9 5 7 1

8. 1990: __ __ __ __ __ __ __ __ __ __ were no longer in power in Soviet Union.
   3 15 13 13 21 14 9 19 20 19

9. 1990: Iraq invaded __ __ __ __ __ __ .
   11 21 23 1 9 20

10. 1990: Bush sent __ __ __ __ __ __ to Saudi Arabia.
    20 18 15 15 16 19

11. 1991: Gen. __ __ __ __ __ __ __ __ __ __ led U.S. forces against Iraq in the Persian Gulf war; air attacks began.
    19 3 8 23 1 18 26 11 15 16 6

12. 1991: Iraq agreed to __ __ __ __ __ terms.
    16 5 1 3 5

13. U.S. gave Russia a __ __ __ __ __ of $1.5 billion dollars.
    12 15 1 14

14. 1992: Noriega was found guilty of drug charges and was sent to __ __ __ __ __ __ .
    16 18 9 19 15 14

15. 1992: Riots began in Los Angeles after a black man, Rodney King, was beaten by four white policemen who were given verdict of not __ __ __ __ __ __ when tried.
    7 21 9 12 20 25

16. 1992: __ __ __ __ __ __ __ elected pres. and Gore, vice-pres.
    3 12 9 14 20 15 14

17. 1992: U.S. invaded __ __ __ __ __ __ __ with U.N. approval.
    19 15 13 1 12 9 1

18. 1993: Clinton __ __ __ __ __ __ __ __ __ __ president.
    9 14 1 21 7 21 18 1 20 5 4

19. George and Barbara retired to __ __ __ __ __ .
    20 5 24 1 19

A - 1	N - 14
B - 2	O - 15
C - 3	P - 16
D - 4	Q - 17
E - 5	R - 18
F - 6	S - 19
G - 7	T - 20
H - 8	U - 21
I - 9	V - 22
J - 10	W - 23
K - 11	X - 24
L - 12	Y - 25
M - 13	Z - 26

123

William J. Clinton
1993–2001

CROSSWORD PUZZLE

ACROSS

1. 1964: Bill entered _____ University in VA.
2. 1976: He became _____ General of Arkansas. (law)
3. Georgetown University: He won a Rhodes Scholarship to study in _____. (country)
6. Bill's birth name: William _____ Blythe IV
8. As a student, Bill drove 200 miles each weekend to visit his stepfather, dying of _____.
12. Nickname: _____
13. His birth father's name: _____
15. When Bill was 4, his mother married Roger Clinton, a _____ salesman. (auto)
16. Before Bill was born, his birth father was _____ in a car accident.
19. Bill lived with his _____ four years while his mother finished nursing school. (mother's parents)
21. Bill was very _____. (bright)
23. Many soldiers were killed in the _____ War. (Asia)
24. 1975: Bill and Hillary were _____.

DOWN

1. Grandfather Cassidy owned a _____ store. (food)
2. Birth state: _____
4. When he was 4, two boys pulled a jumping rope tight, causing Bill to break his _____ in three places.
5. At 7, read the _____ every day. (periodical)
7. Mother, Virginia, studied _____ in New Orleans. (care of sick)
9. Grandfather's grocery was located in a nearly all-_____ neighborhood.
10. Mother's name: _____
11. On the farm, Bill was _____ by a ram and his head was cut open.
14. Was _____ of his classes. (chief)
17. Grandfather treated black customers _____ and respectfully. (warmly)
18. 1968: Took groceries to help the _____ after the Watts riots. (unhoused)
20. Bill treated others with _____ and was well-liked. (esteem)
22. When Bill was 4, his stepfather bought a _____. (country place)

124

William J. Clinton
1993–2001

SUPPLY THE VOWEL

DIRECTIONS

In the grid, look for the following words (the words that are not in parentheses). The words can go up, down, across, at angles, backward, or forward. Parts of words may overlap. Supply the correct vowel—a e i o u—for the center of each word group.

(born) **August** (19, 1946)

(when Bill got excited he cried "hot) **dog**(")

(at the university, he worked two part-time) **jobs** (for Sen. Fulbright)

(1968: Martin Luther) **King** (Jr., was assassinated leading to terrible race riots)

(1970: Bill got a scholarship to Yale) **Law** (School)

(at Yale, Bill met) **Hillary** (Rodham and started to date her)

(Bill and Hillary worked for Sen. McGovern's) **campaign** (for pres.)

```
C I F O B H L A M D K E S
P G C N P Q O S U L C S J
R V Z H R N R E Y W O L T
P R O F O S S O R P M W Y
W A E R S L I C M G P K B
P R D N I U S T H L A F J
V E B W D A O E H Y I D S
F R O I E G M J A O G C P
R O S N N V A T G M N U K
B N A F C S L N E L J C W
Y R I G Y H O L L A R Y D
K E N L H K A X P N M R O
J V G J S Y V A C A U B T
W O R K I N G E B B S G H
D G B D J W A U G O S T F
E N C S I S K R V C S I L
T D O G B M F U A H W H P
```

(at 22: he was) **six** (feet, 2 inches tall)

(1973: was) **professor** (at the U. of Arkansas)

(Janet) **Reno** (was first woman Attorney General)

(Bill debated George) **Bush** (and Ross Perot on TV)

(1979: Bill became) **governor** (of Arkansas)

(1980: almost 20,000) **Cuban** (refugees rioted at Ft. Chaffee, AR)

(1980: baby) **Chelsea** (born)

(1983: Hillary, a) **lawyer**, (worked hard to get Bill elected to office again)

(1985: Arkansas teachers had to) **pass** (tests)

(1991: his program helped many welfare recipients to start) **working**

(1992: Bill campaigned for) **presidency**

(1993: problems with warlords in) **Somalia**

(many governors believed Bill was the best) **U.S.** (gov.)

125

William J. Clinton
1993–2001

SKYSCRAPER
DIRECTIONS
Write your answers in the boxes. The circled letters will help you.

1. Abbr. for Arkansas, Clinton's home state
2. 1993: He signed a _____ (weapon) control bill.
3. He wanted to cut health-_____ costs.
4. 1994: He signed an anti-_____ bill. (assault)
5. 1993: Signed a bill for family and _____ leave. (sick)
6. 1993: Gen. Colin _____ retired as chairman of the Joint Chiefs of Staff.
7. Marines landed in Haiti and helped restore _____ as leader.
8. 1994: U.S. farmers had a record _____ of corn and soybeans. (autumn)
9. 1995: A terrorist bomb killed many in _____. (Midwest state)
10. Moslem terrorists were _____ for the World Trade Center bombing.
11. 1997: _____ cloned two sheep. (those in science)
12. 1993: Bill wanted an _____ reform bill. (foreign people into U.S.)
13. 1993: At 46, Bill was _____ president.

SAME FIRST LETTER
DIRECTIONS
Find two words that begin with the same letter for each of these letters. The circled letter is the first letter for each answer.

Example:
B
B O S N I A — War in ____ continued.
B O R D E R — Iraq troops headed toward the Kuwait ____.

D
1994: Bill's mother ___.
The Senate began ____ on campaign financing laws.

S
Bill ____ the welform reform bill.
The U.S. ____ market crashed.

C
1997: McVeigh was ____ in Oklahoma bombing.
The U.S. World Trade ____ bombers were convicted.

T
____ crash killed 230 people. (airlines)
A ____ company admitted smoking causes cancer.

P
Clinton was reelected ____.
Troops in ____ stormed the Japanese Embassy and rescued hostages.

P
Fund-raising by the Democratic ____ was questioned.
____ Clinton signed a balanced-budget bill.

126

George W. Bush
2001–2009

CROSSWORD PUZZLE

ACROSS
1. George and brothers had two _____. (pets)
2. Had _____ sisters.
3. Maine: George liked boating and catching _____ in the ocean.
6. Father moved his family to _____ in 1948. (state)
7. Father's name: _____ H. W. Bush.
9. Brothers: _____, Neil, and Marvin.
10. Father was a college _____ when George W. was born. (in classes)
12. Family pet: a _____.
15. Born in _____ (state).
16. George W. _____ Laura Welch. (1977, wed)
17. Mother's name: _____.
22. 1952: was in _____ grade in Texas.
23. Wife, Laura, taught _____; later became a librarian.

DOWN
1. Sisters: Robin and _____.
2. Had _____ brothers.
4. Favorite game: _____.
5. Bush family summer home: _____, (Maine).
8. Born: _____ 6, 1946.
10. Liked to play baseball, football, and _____.
11. George's youngest brother: _____.
13. Studied _____ in college. (the past)
14. Sister Robin died when she was _____. (age)
17. High school: went to an academy for _____. (no girls)
18. Father sold oil _____ in Texas.
19. George W. was his mother's first _____.
20. Laura gave birth to _____ girls.
21. George W. ran for governor of Texas and _____.

George W. Bush
2001–2009

SUPPLY THE VOWEL
DIRECTIONS
In the grid, look for the following words (the words that are not in parentheses). The words can go up, down, across, at angles, backward, or forward. Parts of words may overlap. Supply the correct vowel—a e i o u—for the center of each word group.

M	B	F	W	T	Z	K	D	G	I	H	P	J
C	R	○	N	G	E	R	S	F	L	A	M	S
Y	R	M	R	Q	T	X	U	B	D	R	V	P
C	B	I	N	E	D	F	H	D	Y	P	E	J
K	O	L	Q	N	L	T	S	P	○	R	T	
R	Y	Y	A	V	M	Y	W	A	P	R	R	Z
C	E	L	R	R	D	G	F	L	S	H	I	K
J	H	G	○	H	L	K	E	P	H	M	O	N
Q	T	C	U	S	W	V	T	Y	P	Z	A	X
S	H	B	G	J	A	E	F	I	A	E	G	H
R	K	D	O	N	M	E	O	Q	R	M	U	S
C	L	J	V	P	L	N	T	W	G	X	A	P
Y	R	R	○	K	U	Y	P	D	O	S	T	X
A	H	R	R	B	M	O	E	B	T	C	Z	B
V	F	P	N	S	D	N	A	S	○	O	H	T
R	Q	I	O	M	G	S	R	S	A	S	K	W
J	V	T	R	L	U	Z	O	V	N	Q	H	Y

(liked to be with) **people**

(greatest national debt in) **U.S.** (history)

(liked signing) **autographs**

(many people against) **war**

(He had a) **temper**

(ran for) **governor** (of Texas again, and won)

(had many) **rich** (friends)

(terrorist, Osama bin Laden, caused massive deaths in New) **York**

(thousands of National Guard) **troops** (in Iraq war)

(Bush appeared on the) **Oprah** (show)

(was a good) **family** (man)

(helped to buy the Texas) **Rangers** (baseball team)

(many terrorists in) **Iraq**

Bush (was junior high school quarterback for his team)

(brother) **Jeb** (won second race for governor)

high (school: was cheer leader)

barely (won race against Al Gore for president)

(won race against John) **Kerry** (for president)

(made friends) **easily**

thousands (of troops sent to Iraq and Afghanistan)

128

George W. Bush
2001–2009

CROSSING OVER

DIRECTIONS
Use a pencil for this game. Find words from the following list that have the correct number of spaces and letters to fit into the crossing-over boxes (the words not in parentheses). Each word has a place where it belongs. The first word is done for you. To continue, find an eight-letter word having an "A" in the sixth space. All the words tell about George W. Bush.

3 letters
(President's own airplane: Air Force) **one**

4 letters
(Laura Bush liked to) **read** (to children)
(Many coalition forces fought in) **Iraq**
(First term, ran against Al) **Gore** (for president)
(White House has a swimming) **pool**

5 letters
(He cut) **taxes** (to help the economy)
(Sept. 11, 2001: planes hit World) **Trade** (Center)
White (House: President's home)
(1975: worked in the) **Texas** (oil business)

6 letters
(Wife Laura taught) **school**
(President's White House workroom: Oval) **Office**
Secret (Service Agents guard the President)
Father (had been a U.S. president, also)
(George W. chose Dick) **Cheney** (as Vice-President)
(chose Gen. Colin) **Powell** (as Secretary of State)
(bought land and) **cattle** (in Texas)

7 letters
(brother Jeb: Governor of) **Florida**
(lifted) **weights** (to stay strong)
(Bush twins liked) **bowling** (in the White House)

8 letters
(worked to make the) **military** (strong)
(owned part of Texas Rangers) **baseball** (team)

9 letters
(Bush–Gore race for president close: many votes) **recounted**
(George worked hard to fight) **terrorism**
(He met with leaders of other) **countries**
(learned to fly) **airplanes** (for the National Guard)
(2001: became) **President** (of the United States)

10 letters
terrorists (do bad things)

11 letters
(some coalition forces fought in) **Afghanistan**

Answer Key

George Washington
CROSSWORD PUZZLE

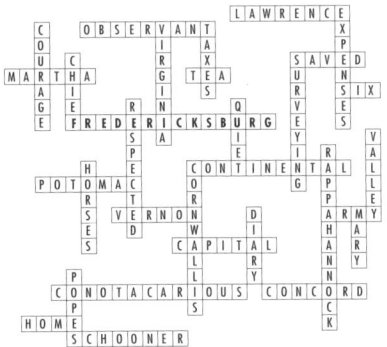

CROSSING OVER

NAME A PLACE WHERE WASHINGTON AND TROOPS NEARLY STARVED AND FROZE

1. **M**artha
2. C**O**rnwallis
3. fi**R**st
4. bi**R**thday
5. k**I**ng
6. pre**S**ident
7. fa**T**her
8. C**O**ncord
9. **W**on
10. Fre**N**ch
11. Co**N**tinental
12. **J**oined

(Morristown, NJ)

SKYSCRAPER

1. six
2. short
3. acres
4. bacon
5. apples
6. bricks
7. dinner
8. miller
9. chickens
10. blacksmith

John Adams
CROSSWORD PUZZLE

WORD SEARCHING

NUMBER CODE

1. defending
2. inaugurated
3. moved, mansion
4. finished, room, moved
5. hung, washing, room
6. Continental
7. Boston

JOHN AND ABIGAIL ADAMS HOME PAIRS

pies	cheese
bread	visits
candles	Braintree
soup	weave
soap	spin
puddings	knit
Bible	sew
church	cook
vegetables	churn
fireplace	herbs

Word that appears once: read

Thomas Jefferson
CROSSWORD PUZZLE

131

Answer Key

SUPPLY THE VOWEL

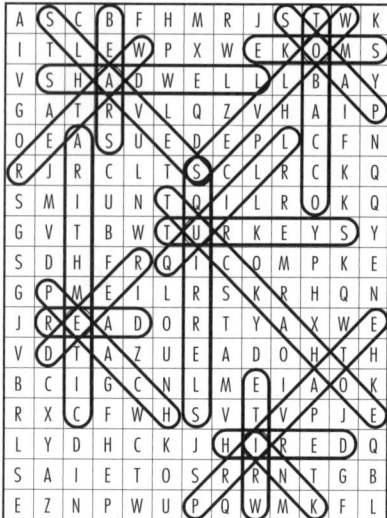

SAME FIRST LETTER

Mary	Tomato
Martha	Turkey
Shadwell	Lawyer
Soap	Land
Pen	Surveyor
Pirates	Slaves
April	Monticello
Apple	Martha

CLUE

1. horses, cattle, hogs
2. mockingbird
3. fat, soap
4. smokehouse
5. apple, peach

James Madison
CROSSWORD PUZZLE

CROSSING OVER

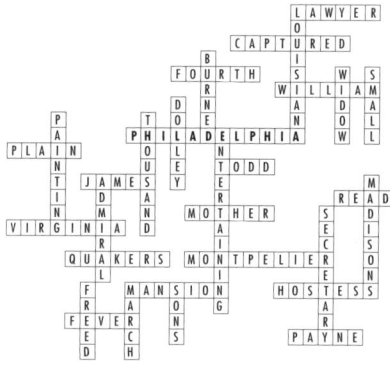

NAME HER HOME PLANTATION

1. Silk
2. briCks
3. hOrses
4. sTeps
5. Cows
6. PHiladelphia
7. preTty
8. AarOn
9. Wagons
10. rolliNg
11. oVer
12. creAm

(Scotchtown, VA)

SCRAMBLED WORDS

1. drapes, clock, silver, portrait, original
2. farmers
3. buried

James Monroe
CROSSWORD PUZZLE

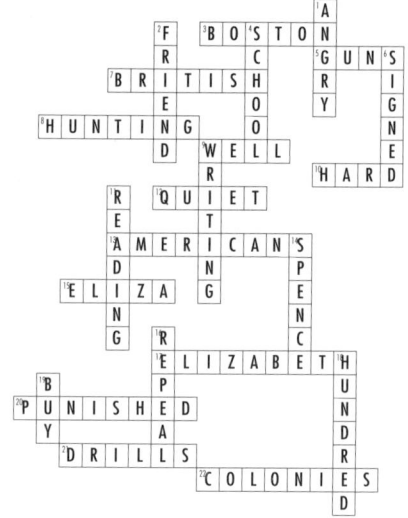

WORD SEARCHING

BOYHOOD FARM PAIRS

tools	turnips
rifles	potatoes
horses	squash
geese	parsnips
chickens	pillows
pigs	quilts
cows	mattresses
milk	tables
butter	chairs
cheese	chests
eggs	cabinets

Word that appears once: gunpowder

132

Presidential Puzzlers Copyright © 2005 Good Year Books

Answer Key

MONROE DOCTRINE
NUMBER CODE

republics, Congress
1. monarchies
2. future
3. intent
4. wars

John Quincy Adams
CROSSWORD PUZZLE

SUPPLY THE VOWEL

CLUE

1. French
2. John
3. married
4. czar
5. jewels
6. state
7. president
8. Potomac
9. Bible
10. oak
11. Smithsonian

WORD IN WORDS

Answers will vary.

Andrew Jackson
CROSSWORD PUZZLE

CROSSING OVER

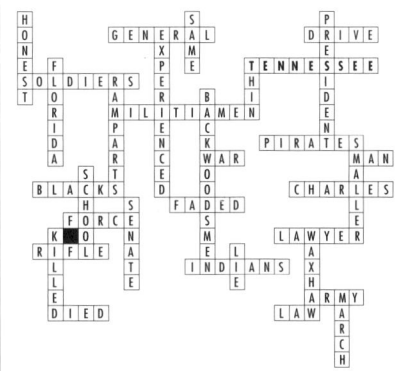

NAME THE PLACE WHERE ANDREW JACKSON STUDIED LAW

1. Jack**S**on
2. l**A**wyer
3. Caro**L**ina
4. Nashv**I**lle
5. ca**S**es
6. **B**ought
7. J**U**dge
8. **R**achel
9. happ**Y**

10. N**C**
11. **C**arolina

(Salisbury, NC)

SKYSCRAPER

1. Old
2. House
3. Adams
4. died
5. horse
6. Indians
7. Mexico
8. slavery
9. tuberculosis

Martin Van Buren
CROSSWORD PUZZLE

133

Answer Key

WORD SEARCHING

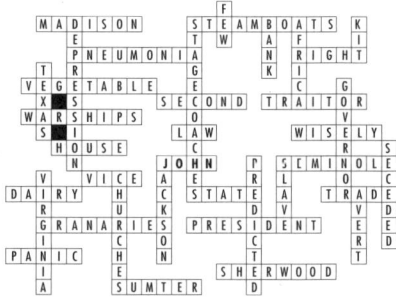

MARTIN'S PRESIDENCY PAIRS

carriage	cannon
eighth	unpopular
riots	treasury
paper money	Congress
disaster	money
banks	gold
panic	elections
anger	withdraw
hunger	economic
mob	Texas

Word that appears once: defeated

SCRAMBLED WORDS

1. second
2. eighth
3. Bank
4. wisely
5. economy
6. hungry
7. reelected

William H. Harrison
CROSSWORD PUZZLE

SUPPLY THE VOWEL

NAME THE FORT THAT WAS DIFFERENT IN ONE WAY

1. Ca**P**tain
2. Grous**E**land
3. **T**ippecanoe
4. **T**imbers
5. **I**ndiana
6. **C**losed
7. w**O**men
8. esc**A**pe
9. **T**ecumseh

(Fort Petticoat was defended by women.)

NUMBER CODE

1. ninth president
2. inaugurated, March
3. two hours, longest
4. cold, wet
5. wife was ill at their home up north
6. caught a cold
7. he was very sick
8. died of pneumonia

John Tyler
CROSSWORD PUZZLE

CROSSING OVER

SAME FIRST LETTER

Philadelphia	Letitia
Pennsylvania	Lawyer
Virginia	Covered Wagons
Vegetables	Corn
Telegraph	Fremont
Tobacco	Florida

ALPHABET SEARCH

Answers will vary.

Answer Key

James K. Polk
CROSSWORD PUZZLE

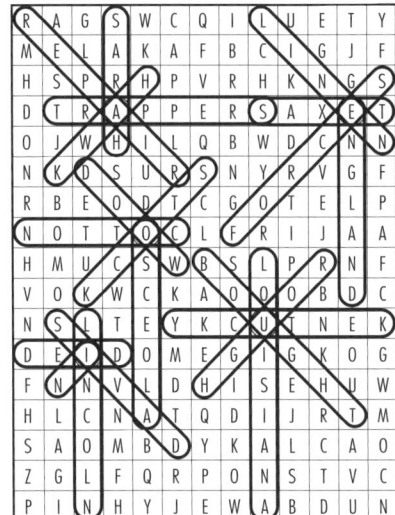

WORD SEARCHING

NUMBER CODE
1. slavery
2. hostess
3. worked, ill
4. Smithsonian
5. card
6. Treasury
7. Oregon
8. secretary
9. Texas, Iowa
10. second

SINGLE-LETTER WORDS
Answers will vary.

Zachary Taylor
CROSSWORD PUZZLE

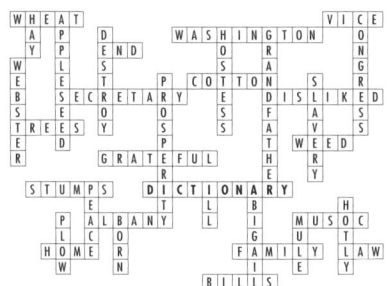

SUPPLY THE VOWEL

SKYSCRAPER
1. well
2. like
3. Nancy
4. cotton
5. Senate
6. Union
7. typhoid
8. Fillmore
9. Whitey
10. Kentucky

NUMBER CODE
In 1850, the first overland mail service began. It went from Missouri to New Mexico.

Millard Fillmore
CROSSWORD PUZZLE

CROSSING OVER

NAME THE BILL
1. en**C**ouraged
2. h**O**rses
3. ter**M**
4. **P**orts
5. Slave**R**y
6. c**O**untries
7. Fill**M**ore's
8. M**I**llard
9. **S**ad
10. ann**E**xed

11. Car**O**lyn
12. Bu**F**falo

(Compromise of 1850)

CLUE
1. bathtub
2. inauguration
3. Civil
4. medicine

135

Answer Key

5. stroke
6. second

Franklin Pierce
CROSSWORD PUZZLE

WORD SEARCHING

SAME FIRST LETTER

Sixty-four — Cabin
Stowe — Concord, NH

Train — Unscrupulous
Trade — Underground

Brown — Kansas
Bitter — Killed

NUMBER CODE
1. cane, nearly killed, three years
2. Buchanan, not Pierce
3. very ill, died, train accident
4. Europe for three years, died in

James Buchanan
CROSSWORD PUZZLE

SUPPLY THE VOWEL

SCRAMBLED WORDS
1. system
2. paper
3. prison
4. advice
5. taken
6. Sumter

HOME AND SCHOOL PAIRS

knit — Latin
cook — college
spin — squirrels
weave — store
sew — trading post
reading — diary
writing — prosperous
math — accounts
English — Mercersburg
Greek — brickhouse

Word that appears once: God

Abraham Lincoln
CROSSWORD PUZZLE

CROSSING OVER

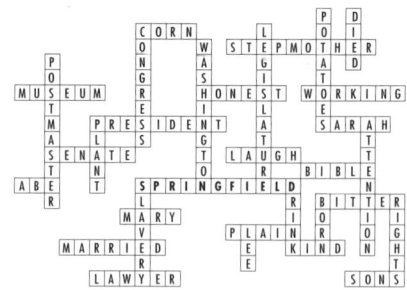

Presidential Puzzlers Copyright © 2005 Good Year Books

136

Answer Key

HOW LINCOLN FELT ABOUT THE SOUTH

1. War
2. SprIngfield
3. RoberT
4. montHs

5. Man
6. EdwArd
7. WilLiam
8. I ll
9. sucCessful
10. honEst

11. elecTed
12. wOn
13. Wrong
14. DouglAs
15. CaRolina
16. presiDent

17. WashiNgton
18. plOt
19. iNaugurated
20. sixtEenth

(with malice toward none)

Andrew Johnson
CROSSWORD PUZZLE

WORD SEARCHING

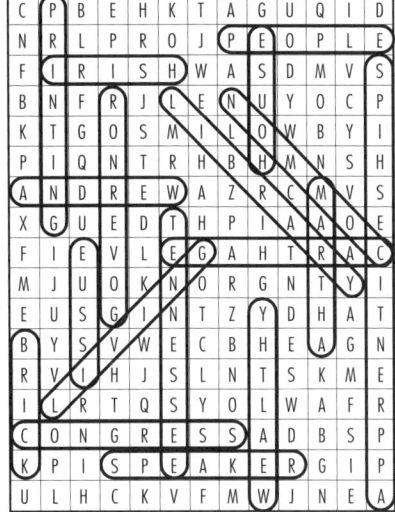

WAR YEARS SKYSCRAPER

1. seven
2. Davis
3. fired
4. Union
5. Governor
6. Charles
7. slaves
8. Johnson
9. president

CLUE

1. tuberculosis
2. hostess
3. mended, milked
4. South, kindness
5. background
6. Ku Klux Klan
7. reconstruction
8. impeach
9. Ulysses S. Grant
10. U.S. Senate
11. U.S. flag, Greeneville, Tennessee

Ulysses S. Grant
CROSSWORD PUZZLE

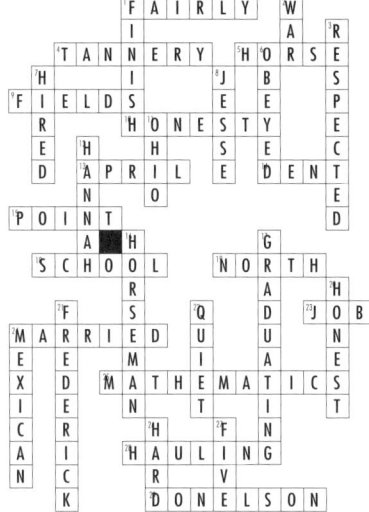

SUPPLY THE VOWEL

SAME FIRST LETTER

Terrorized · Voting
Troops · Very

South · Debt
Spoils · Dishonest

Rights · England
Robes · Europe

137

Answer Key

SCRAMBLED WORDS
1. Europe
2. cheered
3. welcomed
4. parade
5. home, New York
6. book, life

Rutherford B. Hayes
CROSSWORD PUZZLE

CROSSING OVER

RUTHERFORD'S AND FANNY'S CHILDHOOD PAIRS

reading · fishing
writing · swimming
spelling · ice skating
farm · baseball
candy · painting
stories · rifle shooting
games · chess
hiding · laughing
affection · minnows
sports · brook

Word that appears once: tricks

ALPHABET SEARCH
Answers will vary.

James A. Garfield
CROSSWORD PUZZLE

WORD SEARCHING

CLUE
1. bullet, found
2. Garfield died
3. seven, death
4. Lucretia
5. children

NAME THE FARM
1. ELiza
2. blAck
3. Whooping
4. MeNtor
5. Finished
6. traIn
7. rEspect
8. eLected
9. inaugurateD

(Lawnfield)

Chester A. Arthur
CROSSWORD PUZZLE

SUPPLY THE VOWEL

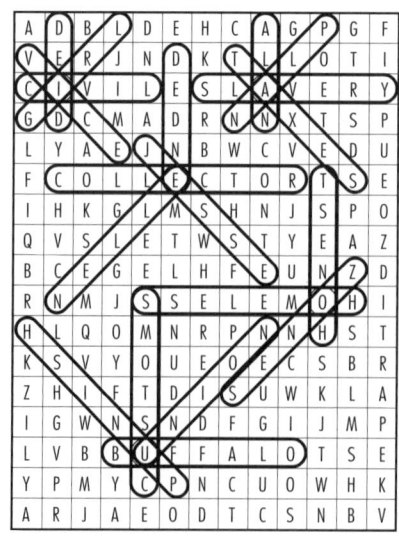

138

Answer Key

SKYSCRAPER

1. VT
2. six
3. two
4. Mary
5. plumbing
6. elevator
7. renovated
8. pneumonia
9. inaugurated
10. tuberculosis

NUMBER CODE

1. shot, president
2. Nell, Alan
3. loved, fish
4. limited
5. exams, government jobs
6. kidney sickness
7. died
8. buried, Albany

Grover Cleveland
CROSSWORD PUZZLE

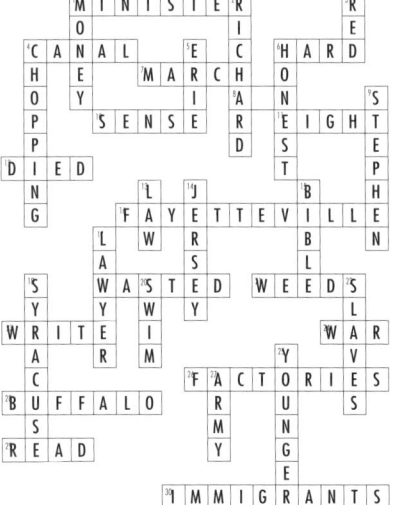

CROSSING OVER

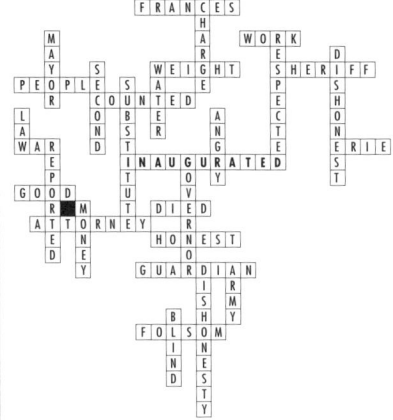

SAME FIRST LETTER

Governor Fairly
Good   Frances

Hours   Teacher
Hostess   Twenty

Married   Workers
Money   Waste

SCRAMBLED WORDS

1. Blue Room
2. Band
3. bells rang
4. guns, Navy
5. house
6. View
7. dinners
8. Statue
9. farmers'
10. waste

Benjamin Harrison
CROSSWORD PUZZLE

WORD SEARCHING

SKYSCRAPER

1. OH
2. war
3. army
4. Senate
5. tariffs
6. President
7. Treasury
8. depression
9. tuberculosis
10. reelection

139

Answer Key

PAIRS

Union	grandchildren
war	honest
hero	work
energy	Republican
Senate	church
tariff	tuberculosis
President	summer
dedication	Mary
speeches	Elizabeth
Indianapolis	died

Word that appears once: pneumonia

Grover Cleveland (Second Term)
CROSSWORD PUZZLE

SUPPLY THE VOWEL

NAME GROVER'S SUMMER HOME LOCATION

1. **B**aby
2. Stat**U**e
3. **Z**ones
4. **Z**ip
5. w**A**ste
6. fa**R**mers'
7. secon**D**
8. depre**S**sion
9. pro**B**lems
10. diptheri**A**
11. Jerse**Y**
12. proble**M**s
13. we**A**k

(Buzzard's Bay, MA)

ALPHABET SEARCH
Answers will vary.

William McKinley
CROSSWORD PUZZLE

CROSSING OVER

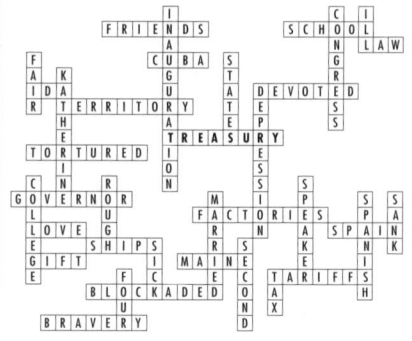

NUMBER CODE

1. sank, ships, Cuba
2. Puerto Rico
3. Guam, Philippines
4. Governor
5. China, trade
6. Governor
7. inaugurated again
8. train trip
9. Pan American Exposition
10. greet, Temple, Music
11. was shot
12. died
13. Theodore Roosevelt, twenty-sixth
14. assassin, electric chair
15. Canton

Theodore Roosevelt
CROSSWORD PUZZLE

140

Answer Key

WORD SEARCHING

SCRAMBLED WORDS

1. Anna, Corinne
2. tact
3. "White House"
4. Panama Canal
5. completed
6. yellow fever
7. again

CLUE

1. hard
2. business
3. married
4. Nobel Peace
5. bears, Teddy Bears
6. capable
7. insane
8. World War
9. killed
10. died, blood clot
11. carved

William H. Taft
CROSSWORD PUZZLE

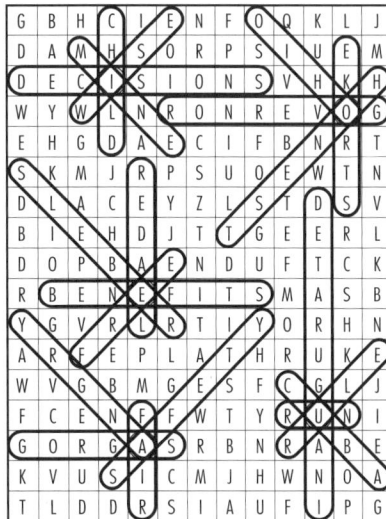

SUPPLY THE VOWEL

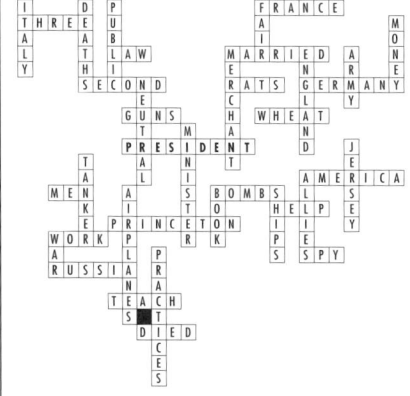

SAME FIRST LETTER

Boy   Pole
Big   President

Automobiles   Scouts
After   Stroke

Titanic   Robert
Temporary   Republican

SKYSCRAPER

1. OH
2. war
3. arms
4. hours
5. night
6. mines
7. Wilson
8. Yale
9. stroke
10. people
11. Supreme
12. seventy

Woodrow Wilson
CROSSWORD PUZZLE

CROSSING OVER

141

Answer Key

WORLD WAR I PAIRS

dugouts	bombs
rats	drafted
balloons	dead
rifles	wounded
machine guns	explosions
submarines	ships
torpedoes	airplanes
Yanks	infantry
troops	Allies

Word that appears once: Armistice

NAME THE GOVERNOR'S HOME

1. **S** ank
2. draft **E** d
3. w **A** r
4. su **G** ar
5. un **I** forms
6. c **R** ops
7. fac **T** ories
8. wou **N** ded
9. **J** ohn

(Sea Girt, NJ)

Warren G. Harding
CROSSWORD PUZZLE

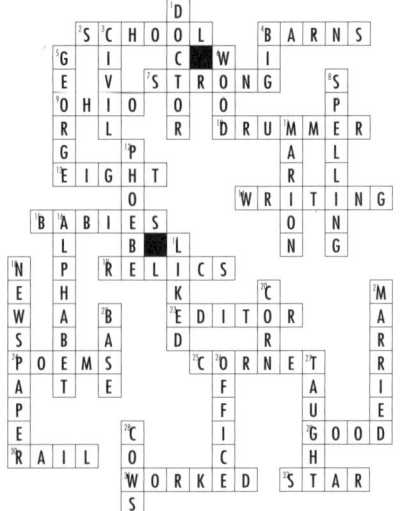

WORD SEARCHING

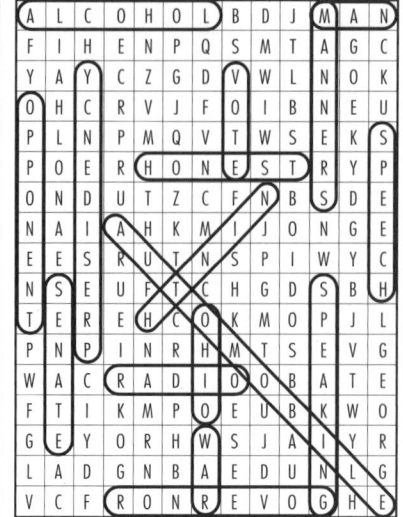

NUMBER CODE

1. car
2. ball, expense
3. Germany
4. body, tomb
5. Arlington
6. listened, changes
7. balanced budget
8. farmers, miners
9. work
10. soldiers
11. White
12. died

Calvin Coolidge
CROSSWORD PUZZLE

SUPPLY THE VOWEL

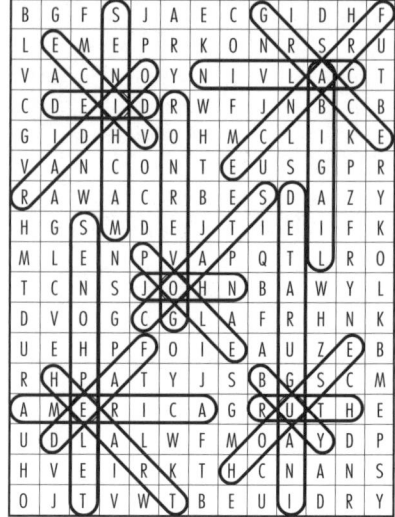

SCRAMBLED WORDS

1. Taft, oath
2. drinks
3. Atlantic
4. pets
5. taxes, debt
6. Hoover
7. president
8. heart
9. buried

NUMBER CODE

1. lowered taxes, U.S. debt down
2. did not want to run for president the second time
3. liked to joke, took a nap. When a servant awakened him, Is the country still here
4. very quiet man, listened, everything, spoken

Answer Key

Herbert C. Hoover
CROSSWORD PUZZLE

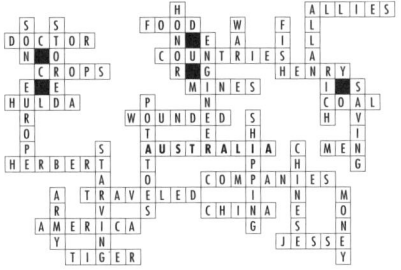

CROSSING OVER

SKYSCRAPER
1. IA
2. TV
3. dam
4. good
5. Hoover
6. market
7. jobs
8. money
9. factories
10. closed
11. Depression

CLUE
1. Roosevelt
2. Boulder
3. money
4. bombed Pearl Harbor
5. World War
6. Germany
7. died, heart
8. Truman
9. White House
10. food supplies
11. millions
12. Hoover
13. Eisenhower
14. died

Franklin D. Roosevelt
CROSSWORD PUZZLE

WORD SEARCHING

NAME THE ROOSEVELTS' SUMMER HOME AND LOCATION
1. **C**ousin
2. H**A**rvard
3. **M**arried
4. Euro**P**e
5. Y**O**rk
6. **B**orn
7. int**E**lligent
8. **L**aw
9. he**L**p
10. Wils**O**n
11. Ass**I**stant
12. stro**N**g
13. inspe**C**t
14. **A**merica
15. Fra**N**klin
16. br**A**ces
17. crashe**D**
18. b**A**nks

(Campobello in Canada)

Harry S. Truman
CROSSWORD PUZZLES

Answer Key

SUPPLY THE VOWEL

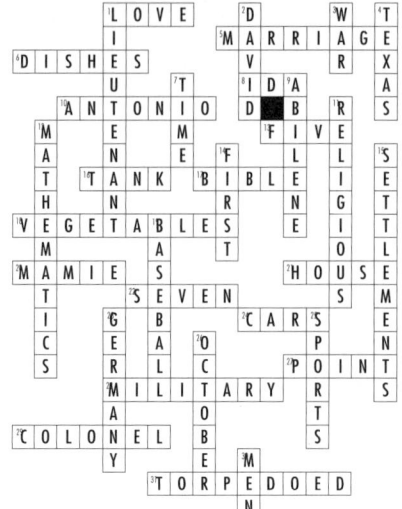

SAME FIRST LETTER

Control
Cabinet

Plane
President

Russia
Road

Reelected
Rosenberg

Army
Aid

Countries
Communists

NUMBER CODE

1. not run for president
2. returned
3. cheered, Kansas City
4. wrote, books
5. walked briskly
6. died
7. buried

Dwight D. Eisenhower
CROSSWORD PUZZLE

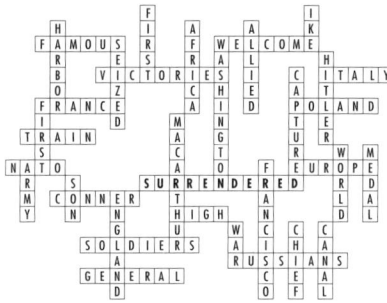

CROSSING OVER

SCRAMBLED WORDS

1. President Nixon
2. leader
3. schools
4. heart
5. King, civil
6. Sputnik
7. submarine
8. farm
9. died
10. Abilene

NUMBER CODE

1. Dwight David
2. Arthur, Edgar, Roy, Earl, Milton
3. Little Ike, Big Ike
4. Doud Dwight, died, scarlet fever
5. second son, John
6. David, Nixon's daughter, Julie

John F. Kennedy
CROSSWORD PUZZLE

WORD SEARCHING

SKYSCRAPER

1. MA
2. you
3. corps
4. Asia
5. Alan
6. moon
7. wall
8. Cuba
9. ships
10. stopped
11. Rights
12. Texas
13. Johnson

Answer Key

CLUE

1. May
2. fever
3. pox
4. read
5. sports
6. sailed
7. London
8. pony
9. Arlington
10. leaders
11. planes, salute

Lyndon B. Johnson
CROSSWORD PUZZLE

SUPPLY THE VOWEL

NAME THE HELICOPTER

1. **C**ourt
2. B**I**rd
3. Sou**T**h
4. Kenned**Y**
5. **F**orce
6. Jaque**L**ine
7. Conne**lY**
8. serv**I**ce
9. **N**ewspaper
10. **G**lycerin
11. **W**ife
12. Pres**I**dent
13. ra**N**
14. Lyn**D**on
15. **M**artin
16. pres**I**dents
17. **L**yndon
18. **L**yndon

([Johnson] City Flying Windmill)

Richard M. Nixon
CROSSWORD PUZZLE

CROSSING OVER

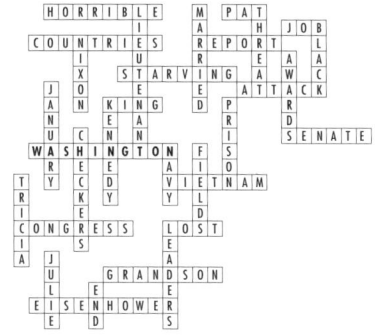

PAIRS

justice	prison
Watergate	Agnew
listening	charges
vandalized	investigation
hotel	impeach
inaugurated	resigned
Democrats	San Clemente
arrested	wrote
five	New Jersey

Word that appears once: died

NUMBER CODE

1. resigned from office
2. recommended impeaching him, justice, presidential, subpoenas
3. almost certain, resigned

Gerald R. Ford
CROSSWORD PUZZLE

Answer Key

WORD SEARCHING

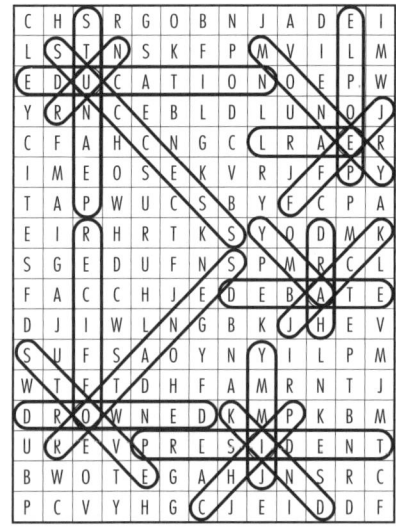

SCRAMBLED WORDS

1. Vietnam
2. Watergate
3. prison
4. guilty
5. Agnew
6. sworn
7. impeach
8. question
9. tapes
10. erased
11. resigned

SKYSCRAPER

1. NE
2. Omaha
3. Ford
4. wrong
5. best
6. invade
7. country
8. women
9. Carter
10. California
11. politics

James E. Carter, Jr.
CROSSWORD PUZZLE

SUPPLY THE VOWEL

NAME THE GROUP THAT WORKED HARD TO ELECT CARTER PRESIDENT

1. **P**icture
2. D**E**mocratic
3. C**A**rter
4. pla**N**
5. q**U**estions
6. no**T**
7. **B**oots
8. P**R**imary
9. Flor**I**da
10. **G**rinning
11. Mond**A**le
12. **D**ebates
13. Pr**E**sident

(Peanut Brigade)

NUMBER CODE

1. people, fireplace
2. poor, lower
3. Israel, Egypt

Ronald W. Reagan
CROSSWORD PUZZLE

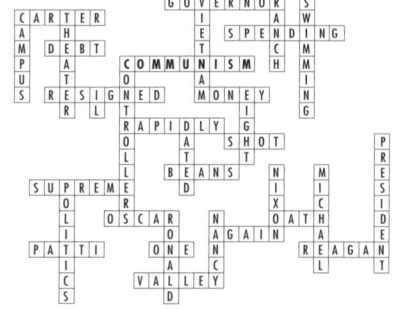

CROSSING OVER

146

Answer Key

PAIRS

Beirut	Libya
Marines	terrorists
killed	Iraq
Communists	oil
Grenada	Kuwait
students	Persian Gulf
paratroopers	NASA
beaches	space
rescue	astronauts
Kaddafi	explosion

Word that appears once: *Challenger*

CLUE

1. drugs, Just Say No
2. George Bush
3. Kaddafi, guns
4. bombed
5. Persian Gulf
6. operation, cancer
7. *Challenger* exploded
8. Gorbachev
9. Bush
10. California

George H. W. Bush
CROSSWORD PUZZLE

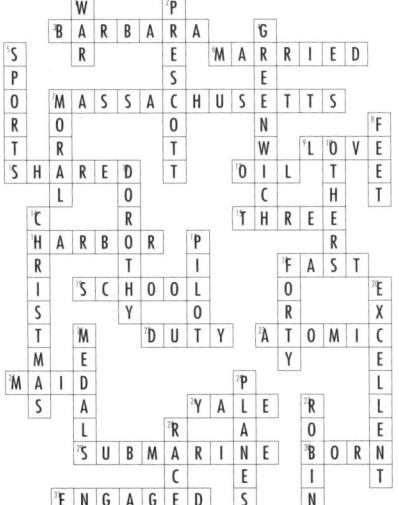

WORD SEARCHING

NUMBER CODE

1. countries
2. Alaska
3. president
4. drugs
5. wall
6. Panama
7. Noriega
8. communists
9. Kuwait
10. troops
11. Schwarzkopf
12. peace
13. loan
14. prison
15. guilty
16. Clinton
17. Somalia
18. inaugurated
19. Texas

William J. Clinton
CROSSWORD PUZZLE

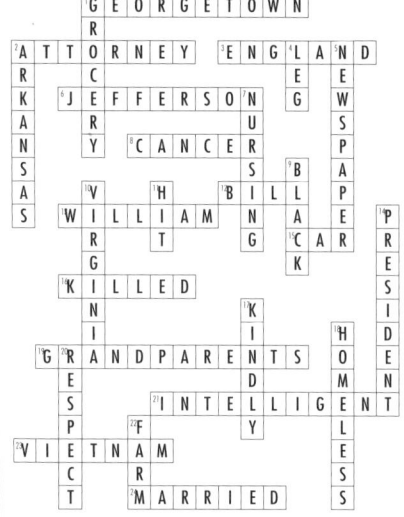

SUPPLY THE VOWEL

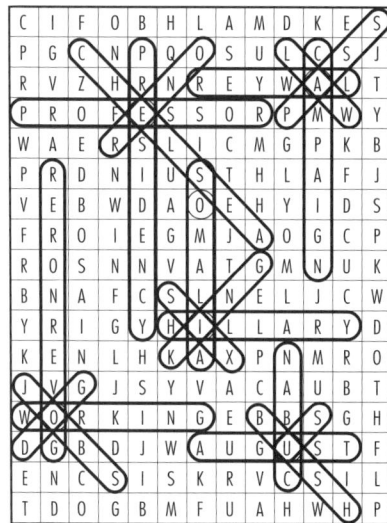

SKYSCRAPER

1. AR
2. gun
3. care
4. crime
5. medical
6. Powell
7. Aristide
8. harvest
9. Oklahoma
10. convicted
11. scientists
12. immigration
13. inaugurated

147

Answer Key

Died   TWA
Debates   Tobacco

Signed   President
Stock   Peru

Convicted   Party
Center   President

GEORGE W. BUSH
CROSSWORD PUZZLE

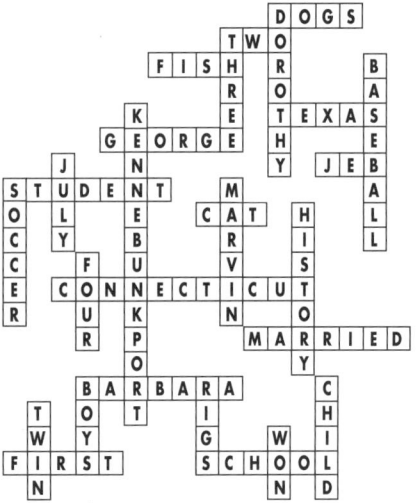

SUPPLY THE VOWEL

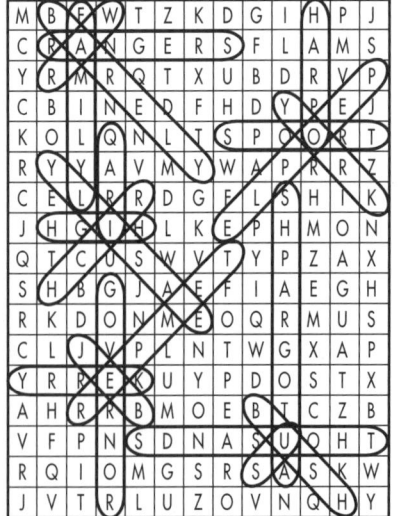

CROSSING OVER

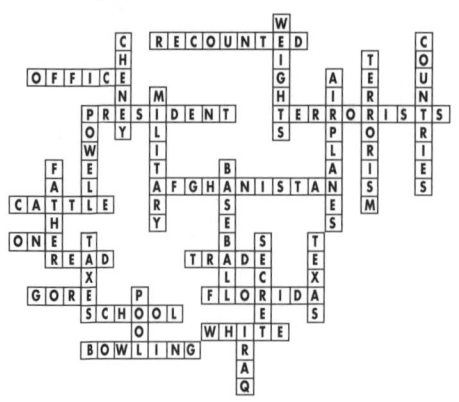

Suggested Reading

George Washington

Adler, David A. *A Picture Book of George Washington.* New York: Holiday House, 1989.

Falkof, Lucille. *George Washington: First President of the United States.* Presidents of the United States series. Ada, OK: Garrett Educational, 1989.

Kent, Zachary. *George Washington.* Encyclopedia of Presidents series. Chicago: Childrens Press, 1986.

Santrey, Laurence. *George Washington: Young Leader.* Mahwah, NJ: Troll Associates, 1986.

John Adams

Santry, Laurence. *John Adams: Brave Patriot.* Mahwah, NJ: Troll Associates, 1986.

Stefoff, Rebecca. *John Adams: Second President of the United States.* Presidents of the United States series. Ada, OK: Garrett Educational, 1988.

Thomas Jefferson

Adler, David A. *Thomas Jefferson: Father of Our Democracy.* A First Biography series. New York: Holiday House, 1987.

Hargrove, Jim. *Thomas Jefferson.* Encyclopedia of Presidents series. Chicago: Childrens Press, 1986.

Stefoff, Rebecca. *Thomas Jefferson: Third President of the United States.* Presidents of the United States series. Ada, OK: Garrett Educational, 1988.

James Madison

Clinton, Susan. *James Madison.* Encyclopedia of Presidents series. Chicago: Childrens Press, 1986.

Fritz, Jean. *The Great Little Madison.* New York: Putnam Publishing Group, 1989.

Quackenbush, Robert. *James Madison and Dolley Madison and Their Times.* New York: Pippin Press, 1992.

James Monroe

Bains, Rae. *James Monroe: Young Patriot.* Mahwah, NJ: Troll Associates, 1986.

Fitz-Gerald, Christine M. *James Monroe.* Encyclopedia of Presidents series. Chicago: Childrens Press, 1987.

Stefoff, Rebecca. *James Monroe: Fifth President of the United States.* Presidents of the United States series. Ada, OK: Garrett Educational, 1988.

John Quincy Adams

Greenblatt, Miriam. *John Quincy Adams: Sixth President of the United States.* Presidents of the United States series. Ada, OK: Garrett Educational, 1990.

Kent, Zachary. *John Quincy Adams.* Encyclopedia of Presidents series. Chicago: Childrens Press, 1987.

Andrew Jackson

Sabin, Louis. *Andrew Jackson: Frontier Patriot.* Mahwah, NJ: Troll Associates, 1986.

Viola, Herman J. *Andrew Jackson.* World Leaders Past and Present series. New York: Chelsea House, 1986.

Martin Van Buren

Ellis, Rafaela. *Martin Van Buren: Eighth President of the United States.* Presidents of the United States series. Ada, OK: Garrett Educational, 1989.

Hargrove, James. *Martin Van Buren.* Encyclopedia of Presidents series. Chicago: Childrens Press, 1987.

William H. Harrison

Fitz-Gerald, Christine. *William Henry Harrison.* Encyclopedia of Presidents series. Chicago: Childrens Press, 1987.

Stefoff, Rebecca. *William Henry Harrison: Ninth President of the United States.* Presidents of the United States series. Ada, OK: Garrett Educational, 1990.

John Tyler

Falkof, Lucille. *John Tyler: Tenth President of the United States.* Presidents of the United States series. Ada, OK: Garrett Educational, 1990.

Lillegard, Dee. *John Tyler.* Encyclopedia of Presidents series. Chicago: Childrens Press, 1987.

James K. Polk

Lillegard, Dee. *James K. Polk.* Encyclopedia of Presidents series. Chicago, Childrens Press, 1988.

Zachary Taylor

Collins, David R. *Zachary Taylor: Twelfth President of the United States.* Presidents of the United States series. Ada, OK: Garrett Educational, 1989.

Kent, Zachary. *Zachary Taylor.* Encyclopedia of Presidents series. Chicago: Childrens Press, 1988.

Millard Fillmore

Casey, Jane C., *Millard Fillmore.* Encyclopedia of Presidents series. Chicago: Childrens Press, 1988.

Law, Kevin J. *Millard Fillmore: Thirteenth President of the United States.* Presidents of the United States series. Ada, OK: Garrett Educational, 1990.

Franklin Pierce

Brown, Fern G. *Franklin Pierce: Fourteenth President of the United States.* Presidents of the United States series. Ada, OK: Garrett Educational, 1989.

Simon, Charnan. *Franklin Pierce. Encyclopedia of Presidents.* Chicago: Childrens Press, 1988.

James Buchanan

Collins, David R. *James Buchanan: Fifteenth President of the United States.* Presidents of the United States series. Ada, OK: Garrett Educational, 1990.

Brill, Marlene T. *James Buchanan.* Encyclopedia of Presidents series. Chicago: Childrens Press, 1988.

Abraham Lincoln

Adler, David A. *Picture Book of Abraham Lincoln.* New York: Holiday House, 1989.

D'Aulaire, Ingri, and Edgar P. D'Aulaire. *Abraham Lincoln.* New York: Doubleday, 1958.

Hargrove, Jim. *Abraham Lincoln.* Encyclopedia of Presidents series. Chicago: Childrens Press, 1988.

Andrew Johnson

Kent, Zachary. *Andrew Johnson.* Encyclopedia of Presidents series. Chicago: Childrens Press, 1989.

Stevens, Rita. *Andrew Johnson: Seventeenth President of the United States.* Presidents of the United States series. Ada, OK: Garrett Educational, 1989.

Ulysses S. Grant

Bentley, Bill. *Ulysses S. Grant.* New York: Franklin Watts, 1993.

Kent, Zachary. *Ulysses S. Grant.* Encyclopedia of Presidents series. Chicago: Childrens Press, 1989.

Rutherford B. Hayes

Kent, Zachary. *Rutherford B. Hayes.* Encyclopedia of Presidents series. Chicago: Childrens Press, 1989.

Robbins, Neal E. *Rutherford B. Hayes: Nineteenth President of the United States.* Presidents of the United States series. Ada, OK: Garrett Educational, 1989.

James A. Garfield

Brown, Fern G. *James A. Garfield: Twentieth President of the United States.* Presidents of the United States series. Ada, OK: Garrett Educational, 1990.

Lillegard, Dee. *James A. Garfield.* Encyclopedia of Presidents series. Chicago: Childrens Press, 1987.

★ ★

Chester A. Arthur

Simon, Charnan. *Chester A. Arthur.* Encyclopedia of Presidents series. Chicago: Childrens Press, 1989.

Grover Cleveland

Collins, David R. *Grover Cleveland: Twenty-second and Twenty-fourth President of the United States.* Presidents of the United States series. Ada, OK: Garrett Educational, 1988.

Kent, Zachary. *Grover Cleveland.* Encyclopedia of Presidents series. Chicago: Childrens Press, 1988.

Benjamin Harrison

Clinton, Susan. *Benjamin Harrison.* Encyclopedia of Presidents series. Chicago: Childrens Press, 1989.

Stins, Richard. *Harrison, Cleveland, McKinley, & Theodore Roosevelt.* Complete History of Our Presidents series. Vero Beach, FL: Rourke, 1996.

William McKinley

Collins, David R. *William McKinley: Twenty-fifth President of the United States.* Presidents of the United States series. Ada, OK: Garrett Educational, 1990.

Kent, Zachary. *William McKinley.* Encyclopedia of Presidents series. Chicago: Childrens Press, 1988.

Theodore Roosevelt

Kent, Zachary. *Theodore Roosevelt.* Encyclopedia of Presidents series. Chicago: Childrens Press, 1988.

Markham, Lois. *Theodore Roosevelt.* World Leaders—Past and Present series. New York: Chelsea House, 1985.

Potts, Steve. *Theodore Roosevelt.* Read—and—Discover Biographies series. Chicago: Childrens Press, 1996.

William H. Taft

Casey, Jane Clark. *William Howard Taft.* Encyclopedia of Presidents series. Chicago: Childrens Press, 1989.

Falkof, Lucille. *William H. Taft: Twenty-seventh President of the United States.* Presidents of the United States series. Ada, OK: Garrett Educational, 1990.

Woodrow Wilson

Osinski, Alice. *Woodrow Wilson.* Encyclopedia of Presidents series. Chicago: Childrens Press, 1989.

Warren G. Harding

Canadeo, Anne. *Warren G. Harding: Twenty-ninth President of the United States.* Presidents of the United States series. Ada, OK: Garrett Educational, 1990.

Wade, Linda. *Warren G. Harding.* Encyclopedia of Presidents series. Chicago: Childrens Press, 1989.

Calvin Coolidge

Kent, Zachary. *Calvin Coolidge.* Encyclopedia of Presidents series. Chicago: Childrens Press, 1988.

Stevens, Rita. *Calvin Coolidge: Thirtieth President of the United States.* Presidents of the United States series. Ada, OK: Garrett Educational, 1990.

Herbert C. Hoover

Clinton, Susan. *Herbert Hoover.* Encyclopedia of Presidents series. Chicago: Childrens Press, 1988.

Polikoff, Barbara G. *Herbert C. Hoover: Thirty-first President of the United States.* Presidents of the United States series. Ada, OK: Garrett Educational, 1990.

Franklin D. Roosevelt

Okinski, Alice. *Franklin D. Roosevelt.* Encyclopedia of Presidents series. Chicago: Childrens Press, 1987.

Potts, Steve. *Franklin D. Roosevelt: A Photo-illustrated Biography.* Mankato, MN: Bridgestone Books, 1996.

Harry S. Truman

Collins, David R. *Harry S. Truman: Thirty-third President of the United States.* Presidents of the United States series. Ada, OK: Garrett Educational, 1985.

Hargrove, Jim. *Harry S. Truman.* Encyclopedia of Presidents series. Chicago: Childrens Press, 1987.

Dwight D. Eisenhower

Hargrove, Jim. *Dwight D. Eisenhower.* Encyclopedia of Presidents series. Chicago: Childrens Press, 1987.

Jacobs, William Jay. *Dwight David Eisenhower.* A First Book series. New York: Franklin Watts, 1995.

John F. Kennedy

Anderson, Catherine C. *John F. Kennedy: Young People's President.* Minneapolis, MN: Lerner Publications, 1991.

Falkof, Lucille. *John F. Kennedy: Thirty-fifth President of the United States.* Presidents of the United States series. Ada, OK: Garrett Educational, 1988.

Potts, Steve. *John F. Kennedy: A Photo-illustrated Biography.* Mankato, MN: Bridgestone Books, 1996.

Lyndon B. Johnson

Falkof, Lucille. *Lyndon B. Johnson: Thirty-sixth President of the United States.* Presidents of the United States series. Ada, OK: Garrett Educational, 1989.

Hargrove, Jim. *Lyndon B. Johnson.* Encyclopedia of Presidents series. Chicago: Childrens Press, 1987.

Richard M. Nixon

Lillegard, Dee. *Richard Nixon.* Encyclopedia of Presidents series. Chicago: Childrens Press, 1988.

Stefoff, Rebecca. *Richard M. Nixon: Thirty-seventh President of the United States.* Presidents of the United States series. Ada, OK: Garrett Educational, 1990.

Gerald R. Ford

Collins, David R. *Gerald R. Ford: Thirty-eighth President of the United States.* Presidents of the United States series. Ada, OK: Garrett Educational, 1990.

Sipiera, Paul P. *Gerald Ford.* Encyclopedia of Presidents series. Chicago: Childrens Press, 1989.

James E. Carter, Jr.

Carrigan, Mellonee. *Jimmy Carter: Beyond His Presidency.* Chicago: Childrens Press, 1989.

Wade, Linda R. *James Carter.* Encyclopedia of Presidents series. Chicago: Childrens Press, 1989.

Ronald W. Reagan

Kent, Zachary. *Ronald Reagan.* Encyclopedia of Presidents series. Chicago: Childrens Press, 1989.

Robbins, Neal E. *Ronald W. Reagan: Fortieth President of the United States.* Presidents of the United States series. Ada, OK: Garrett Educational, 1990.

George H.W. Bush

Kent, Zachary. *George Bush.* Encyclopedia of Presidents series. Chicago: Childrens Press, 1989.

Stefoff, Rebecca. *George H.W. Bush: Forty-first President of the United States.* Presidents of the United States series. Ada, OK: Garrett Educational, 1990.

William J. Clinton

Cole, Michael D. *Bill Clinton: United States President.* People to Know series. Hillside, NJ: Enslow Publishers, 1994.

Cwiklik, Robert. *Bill Clinton: President of the 90's.* A Gateway Biography series. Brookfield, CT: Millbrook Press, 1997.

Landau, Elaine. *Bill Clinton and His Presidency.* A First Book series. New York: Franklin Watts, 1997.

George W. Bush

Cohen, Daniel. *George W. Bush: The family Bussiness.* A Gateway Biography.

Brookfield, CT: The Millbrook Press, 2000.

Gaines, Ann Graham. *George W. Bush: President.* Our Presidents Series.

Chanhassen, MN: The Child's World, 2001.